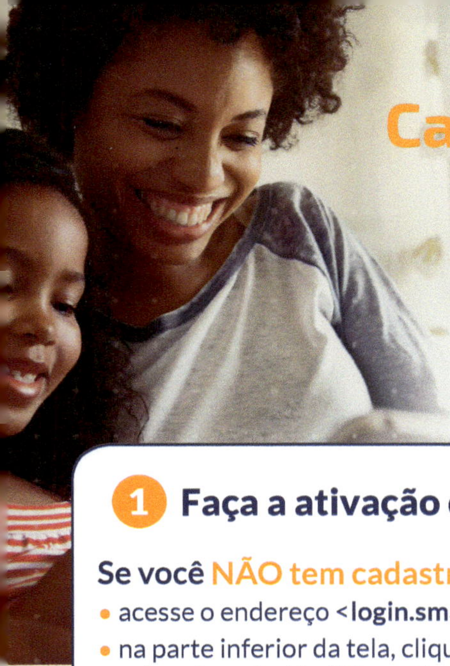

Caro aluno, seja bem-vindo à sua plataforma do conhecimento!

A partir de agora, está à sua disposição uma plataforma que reúne, em um só lugar, recursos educacionais digitais que complementam os livros impressos e foram desenvolvidos especialmente para auxiliar você em seus estudos. Veja como é fácil e rápido acessar os recursos deste projeto.

1 Faça a ativação dos códigos dos seus livros.

Se você NÃO tem cadastro na plataforma:
- acesse o endereço <login.smaprendizagem.com>;
- na parte inferior da tela, clique em "Registre-se" e depois no botão "Alunos";
- escolha o país;
- preencha o formulário com os dados do tutor, do aluno e de acesso.

O seu tutor receberá um *e-mail* para validação da conta. Atenção: sem essa validação, não é possível acessar a plataforma.

Se você JÁ tem cadastro na plataforma:
- em seu computador, acesse a plataforma pelo endereço <login.smaprendizagem.com>;
- em seguida, você visualizará os livros que já estão ativados em seu perfil. Clique no botão "Códigos ou licenças", insira o código abaixo e clique no botão "Validar".

Este é o seu código de ativação! → **DURTT-VASBR-A8GPP**

2 Acesse os recursos

usando um computador.

No seu navegador de internet, digite o endereço <login.smaprendizagem.com> e acesse sua conta. Você visualizará todos os livros que tem cadastrados. Para escolher um livro, basta clicar na sua capa.

usando um dispositivo móvel.

Instale o aplicativo **SM Aprendizagem**, que está disponível gratuitamente na loja de aplicativos do dispositivo. Utilize o mesmo *login* e a mesma senha que você cadastrou na plataforma.

Importante! Não se esqueça de sempre cadastrar seus livros da SM em seu perfil. Assim, você garante a visualização dos seus conteúdos, seja no computador, seja no dispositivo móvel. Em caso de dúvida, entre em contato com nosso canal de atendimento pelo **telefone 0800 72 54876** ou pelo *e-mail* **atendimento@grupo-sm.com**.

BOOK 1

ENGLISH

ENSINO FUNDAMENTAL

LUCIANA RENDA B. DE MELO
Graduada em Pedagogia e Administração de Empresas.
Pós-graduada em Psicopedagogia e Linguística Aplicada a Língua Inglesa.
Diploma de Ensino de Inglês pelo SIT (School for International Training).
Professora de Inglês e pedagoga bilíngue.

MARCELO BACCARIN
Mestre em Educação.
Graduado em Pedagogia (Orientação Educacional) e Letras: Inglês-Português.
Diploma em Ensino de Inglês como Língua Estrangeira (DTEFLA) pela Universidade de Cambridge.
Professor, coordenador e gestor na rede particular de ensino.
Formador de professores e consultor independente em educação e bilinguismo.

RONALDO LIMA JR.
Doutor em Linguística.
Mestre em Linguística Aplicada.
Graduado e Licenciado em Letras – Inglês.
Professor do Departamento de Estudos da Língua Inglesa da Universidade Federal do Ceará.

São Paulo, 2ª edição, 2021

Learning Together 1
© SM Educação
Todos os direitos reservados

Direção editorial Cláudia Carvalho Neves
Gerência editorial Lia Monguilhott Bezerra
Gerência de *design* e produção André Monteiro
Edição executiva Ana Luiza Couto
Edição: Barbara Manholeti, Danuza Gonçalves
Assistência de edição: Natália Feulo do Espírito Santo
Suporte editorial: Fernanda de Araújo Fortunato
Coordenação de preparação e revisão Cláudia Rodrigues do Espírito Santo
Preparação: Andréa Vidal
Revisão: Andréa Vidal
Coordenação de *design* Gilciane Munhoz
***Design*:** Thatiana Kalaes, Lissa Sakajiri
Coordenação de arte Andressa Fiorio
Edição de arte: Fernando Cesar Fernandes
Assistência de arte: Heidy Clemente, Rosangela Cesar de Lima
Assistência de produção: Leslie Morais
Coordenação de iconografia Josiane Laurentino
Pesquisa iconográfica: Ana Stein
Tratamento de imagem: Marcelo Casaro
Capa APIS Design
Ilustração da capa: Henrique Mantovani Petrus
Projeto gráfico APIS Design
Editoração eletrônica Estúdio Type
Pré-impressão Américo Jesus
Fabricação Alexander Maeda
Impressão Forma Certa Gráfica Digital

Em respeito ao meio ambiente, as folhas deste livro foram produzidas com fibras obtidas de árvores de florestas plantadas, com origem certificada.

Dados Internacionais de Catalogação na Publicação (CIP)
(Câmara Brasileira do Livro, SP, Brasil)

Melo, Luciana Renda B. de
 Learning together, 1º ano : ensino fundamental / Luciana Renda B. de Melo, Marcelo Baccarin, Ronaldo Lima Jr. — 2. ed. — São Paulo : Edições SM, 2021. — (Learning together)

 ISBN 978-65-5744-274-6 (aluno)
 ISBN 978-65-5744-304-0 (professor)

 1. Inglês (Ensino fundamental) I. Baccarin, Marcelo. II. Lima Junior, Ronaldo. III. Título. IV. Série.

21-66436 CDD-372.652

Índices para catálogo sistemático:

1. Inglês : Ensino fundamental   372.652

Cibele Maria Dias — Bibliotecária — CRB-8/9427

2ª edição, 2021
5 impressão, outubro 2025

SM Educação
Rua Cenno Sbrighi, 25 – Edifício West Tower n. 45 – 1º andar
Água Branca 05036-010 São Paulo SP Brasil
Tel. 11 2111-7400
atendimento@grupo-sm.com
www.grupo-sm.com/br

APRESENTAÇÃO

CARO(A) ESTUDANTE,

ESTE LIVRO FOI CUIDADOSAMENTE PENSADO PARA AJUDAR VOCÊ A CONSTRUIR UMA APRENDIZAGEM SÓLIDA E CHEIA DE SIGNIFICADOS QUE LHE SEJAM ÚTEIS NÃO SOMENTE HOJE, MAS TAMBÉM NO FUTURO. NELE, VOCÊ VAI ENCONTRAR ESTÍMULOS PARA CRIAR, EXPRESSAR IDEIAS E PENSAMENTOS, REFLETIR SOBRE O QUE APRENDE, TROCAR EXPERIÊNCIAS E CONHECIMENTOS.

OS TEMAS, OS TEXTOS, AS IMAGENS E AS ATIVIDADES PROPOSTOS NESTE LIVRO OFERECEM OPORTUNIDADES PARA QUE VOCÊ SE DESENVOLVA COMO ESTUDANTE E COMO CIDADÃ(O), CULTIVANDO VALORES UNIVERSAIS COMO RESPONSABILIDADE, RESPEITO, SOLIDARIEDADE, LIBERDADE E JUSTIÇA.

ACREDITAMOS QUE É POR MEIO DE ATITUDES POSITIVAS E CONSTRUTIVAS QUE SE CONQUISTAM A AUTONOMIA E A CAPACIDADE PARA TOMAR DECISÕES ACERTADAS, RESOLVER PROBLEMAS E SUPERAR CONFLITOS.

ESPERAMOS QUE ESTE MATERIAL DIDÁTICO CONTRIBUA PARA O SEU DESENVOLVIMENTO E PARA A SUA FORMAÇÃO.

BONS ESTUDOS!

OS AUTORES

CONHEÇA SEU LIVRO

CONHECER SEU LIVRO DIDÁTICO VAI AJUDÁ-LO(A) A APROVEITAR MELHOR AS OPORTUNIDADES DE APRENDIZAGEM QUE ELE OFERECE.

ESTE VOLUME CONTÉM UMA UNIDADE INICIAL DE SEIS PÁGINAS, OITO UNIDADES DE OITO PÁGINAS, DUAS REVISÕES, UM CADERNO DE ATIVIDADES E ALGUMAS SEÇÕES ESPECIAIS.

VEJA COMO CADA PARTE DO SEU LIVRO ESTÁ ORGANIZADA.

ABERTURA DO LIVRO
WELCOME UNIT

VOCÊ JÁ DEVE TER ALGUM CONHECIMENTO DE INGLÊS ADQUIRIDO POR MEIO DE FILMES, MÚSICAS, LIVROS, PROGRAMAS DE TV E PELA INTERNET. NESTA UNIDADE, VOCÊ TERÁ A OPORTUNIDADE DE RESGATAR E TER CONTATO COM O QUE JÁ SABE SOBRE A LÍNGUA INGLESA, ALÉM DE PERCEBER O QUANTO CONHECE SOBRE UM DOS IDIOMAS MAIS USADOS NO MUNDO.

INTRODUÇÃO DA UNIDADE

A UNIDADE COMEÇA COM UMA HISTÓRIA DIVERTIDA QUE ABORDA TEMAS DO COTIDIANO DE CRIANÇAS DA SUA IDADE. A VIDA ESCOLAR, O AMBIENTE FAMILIAR E A CONVIVÊNCIA ENTRE AMIGOS ESTÃO ENTRE OS ASSUNTOS QUE ABRIRÃO AS PORTAS PARA VOCÊ APRENDER NOVAS PALAVRAS, EXPRESSÕES ORAIS E SONS DA LÍNGUA INGLESA.

DESENVOLVIMENTO DO ASSUNTO

OS TEXTOS, AS IMAGENS E AS ATIVIDADES DESTAS PÁGINAS VÃO PERMITIR QUE VOCÊ COMPREENDA O CONTEÚDO QUE ESTÁ SENDO APRESENTADO.

SING ALONG

ESTA SEÇÃO É UMA OPORTUNIDADE PARA VOCÊ INTERAGIR COM O QUE APRENDEU NAS PÁGINAS ANTERIORES. VOCÊ FARÁ ISSO OUVINDO, CANTANDO E DANÇANDO UMA DIVERTIDA MÚSICA EM INGLÊS.

4 FOUR

LANGUAGE CORNER

ALGUMAS PALAVRAS E EXPRESSÕES DA HISTÓRIA DE ABERTURA SERÃO APRESENTADAS E APROFUNDADAS EM ATIVIDADES QUE AJUDARÃO VOCÊ A FALAR, OUVIR, LER E ESCREVER EM INGLÊS.

SOUNDS LIKE FUN

O CONTEÚDO DESTA PÁGINA PERMITIRÁ QUE VOCÊ CONHEÇA OS FONEMAS DA LÍNGUA INGLESA. AO REALIZAR AS ATIVIDADES DE ÁUDIO E PRONÚNCIA, VOCÊ PERCEBERÁ QUE FALAR INGLÊS PODE SER MUITO LEGAL!

PEOPLE WHO CARE

ESTE É O MOMENTO PARA REFLETIR E CONVERSAR COM OS COLEGAS SOBRE COMO TER BOAS PRÁTICAS PARA MELHORAR A CONVIVÊNCIA COM SUA FAMÍLIA, COM A COMUNIDADE ESCOLAR E COM TODOS A SUA VOLTA.

GAMES AND CHALLENGES

NESTA PÁGINA, VOCÊ ENCONTRARÁ JOGOS PARA SE DIVERTIR COM OS COLEGAS, AO MESMO TEMPO QUE INTERAGE E RESGATA O QUE APRENDEU NA UNIDADE.

FIVE 5

FINALIZANDO A UNIDADE

NO FIM DAS UNIDADES, HÁ SEÇÕES QUE BUSCAM AMPLIAR SEUS CONHECIMENTOS SOBRE A LEITURA DE IMAGENS, A DIVERSIDADE CULTURAL E OS CONTEÚDOS ABORDADOS.

LET'S READ IMAGES!

NESTA SEÇÃO VOCÊ VAI APRECIAR E ANALISAR IMAGENS PARA AMPLIAR SEU REPERTÓRIO CULTURAL.

PEOPLE AND PLACES

ESTA SEÇÃO É UM CONVITE PARA VOCÊ CONHECER ALGUMAS CARACTERÍSTICAS CULTURAIS DE DIFERENTES COMUNIDADES.

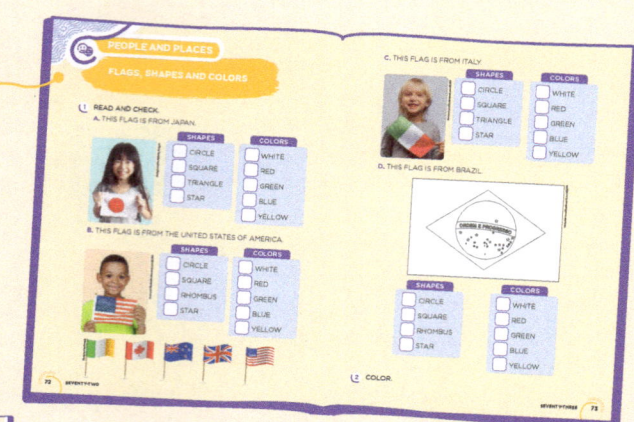

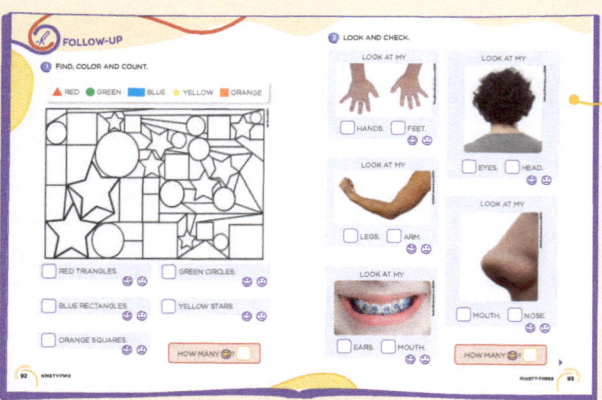

FOLLOW-UP

ESTE ESPAÇO PERMITE QUE VOCÊ REVISE O QUE APRENDEU NAS ÚLTIMAS QUATRO UNIDADES. COM AS ATIVIDADES DESTA SEÇÃO, VOCÊ PODERÁ AVALIAR SE HÁ ALGUM TEMA A SER APERFEIÇOADO E TAMBÉM ACOMPANHAR SEU DESENVOLVIMENTO NAS AULAS DE INGLÊS.

PROJECTS

NESTA SEÇÃO, VOCÊ REALIZARÁ PROJETOS EM GRUPO RELACIONADOS AOS TEMAS DAS UNIDADES. ESSA É UMA BOA OPORTUNIDADE PARA APRENDER A CONVERSAR, OUVIR E COMPARTILHAR EXPERIÊNCIAS E IDEIAS COM OS(AS) COLEGAS.

GLOSSARY

VOCÊ PODERÁ CONSULTAR O GLOSSÁRIO QUANDO SENTIR DIFICULDADE EM COMPREENDER ALGUMA PALAVRA OU EXPRESSÃO USADA NO LIVRO, OU SEMPRE QUE QUISER RELEMBRAR ALGUM CONTEÚDO ESTUDADO.

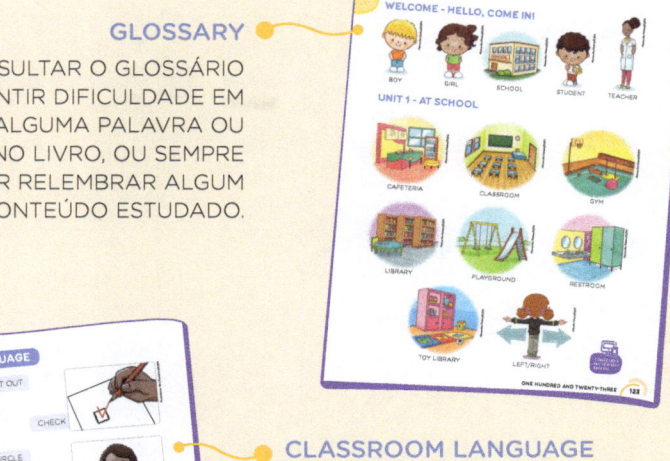

CLASSROOM LANGUAGE

CONSULTE ESTA SEÇÃO PARA SE COMUNICAR EM INGLÊS COM TODOS NA SALA DE AULA.

WORKBOOK

ESTE É UM CADERNO DE ATIVIDADES QUE CONTÉM DESAFIOS ESPECIALMENTE ELABORADOS PARA CADA UNIDADE ESTUDADA. VOCÊ PODERÁ UTILIZÁ-LO EM SALA DE AULA OU COMO LIÇÃO DE CASA.

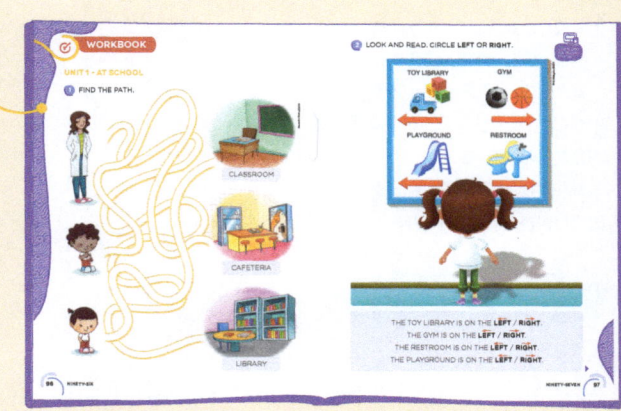

ÍCONES USADOS NO LIVRO

 ATIVIDADE EM DUPLA

 **ATIVIDADE EM GRUPO**

 ATIVIDADE ORAL

 RODA DE CONVERSA

 ÁUDIO
INDICA A FAIXA DE ÁUDIO RELACIONADA À ATIVIDADE.

 MÚSICA
INDICA QUE HÁ UMA MÚSICA RELACIONADA À ATIVIDADE.

 DESTACAR
INDICA QUE HÁ UM DESTACÁVEL NO FINAL DO LIVRO PARA SER UTILIZADO NA ATIVIDADE.

 COLAR
INDICA QUE HÁ ADESIVOS NO FINAL DO LIVRO PARA UTILIZAÇÃO NA ATIVIDADE.

 **VALUES**
INDICA A SEÇÃO *PEOPLE WHO CARE*.

 **OED**
INDICA QUE HÁ UM OBJETO EDUCACIONAL DIGITAL A SER EXPLORADO NO LIVRO DIGITAL.

SEVEN 7

SUMMARY

 WELCOME — HELLO, COME IN! • 10

UNIT 1 — AT SCHOOL • 16
LANGUAGE CORNER
 PLACES AT SCHOOL • 18
 LEFT × RIGHT • 19
SING ALONG
 WELCOME TO SCHOOL • 20
SOUNDS LIKE FUN
 INITIAL SOUND /t/ • 21
PEOPLE WHO CARE
 CARE AND KINDNESS • 22
GAMES AND CHALLENGES
 LABYRINTH • 23

UNIT 2 — SCHOOL STUFF • 24
LANGUAGE CORNER
 SCHOOL OBJECTS • 26
 WHAT'S THIS? • 26
 NUMBERS 1 TO 5 • 27
SING ALONG
 WHAT'S THIS? • 28
SOUNDS LIKE FUN
 INITIAL SOUND /p/ • 29
PEOPLE WHO CARE
 ORGANIZING YOURSELF • 30
GAMES AND CHALLENGES
 SCAVENGER HUNT • 31
PEOPLE AND PLACES
 GOING TO SCHOOL • 32

UNIT 3 — COLORS ALL AROUND • 34
LANGUAGE CORNER
 COLORS • 36
SING ALONG
 WHAT COLOR IS THE SKY? • 38
SOUNDS LIKE FUN
 INITIAL SOUND /r/ • 39
PEOPLE WHO CARE
 ATTENTION • 40
GAMES AND CHALLENGES
 BOARD GAME 1 • 41

UNIT 4 — THE PLAYGROUND • 42
LANGUAGE CORNER
 EXPRESSION: LET'S PLAY! • 44
 PLAYGROUND EQUIPMENTS • 45
 COLORS • 45
SING ALONG
 LET'S PLAY! • 46
SOUNDS LIKE FUN
 INITIAL SOUND /s/ • 47
PEOPLE WHO CARE
 COOPERATION • 48
GAMES AND CHALLENGES
 FIND AND CIRCLE • 49
LET'S READ IMAGES!
 COLORS IN NATURE • 50

 FOLLOW-UP • 52

UNIT 5 — SHAPES AND FUN • 56
LANGUAGE CORNER
 SHAPES AND COLORS • 58
 NUMBERS 6 TO 10 • 59
SING ALONG
 SHAPES SONG • 60
SOUNDS LIKE FUN
 INITIAL SOUND /ʃ/ • 61
PEOPLE WHO CARE
 ATTENTION AND RESPECT • 62
GAMES AND CHALLENGES
 A SHAPE GAME • 63

8 EIGHT

UNIT 6 — MY BODY — 64

LANGUAGE CORNER
MY BODY • 66
SING ALONG
THE HOKEY COKEY • 68
SOUNDS LIKE FUN
INITIAL SOUND /b/ • 69
PEOPLE WHO CARE
HEALTHY HABITS • 70
GAMES AND CHALLENGES
BOARD GAME 2 • 71
PEOPLE AND PLACES
FLAGS, SHAPES AND COLORS • 72

UNIT 7 — MY FAMILY — 74

LANGUAGE CORNER
FAMILY MEMBERS • 76
SING ALONG
THE FINGER FAMILY • 78
SOUNDS LIKE FUN
INITIAL SOUND /f/ • 79
TONGUE TWISTER • 79
PEOPLE WHO CARE
LOVE AND RESPECT • 80
GAMES AND CHALLENGES
DICE FAMILY GAME • 81

UNIT 8 — BREAK TIME — 82

LANGUAGE CORNER
FOOD AND GAMES • 84
LET'S PLAY • 85
SING ALONG
LET'S PLAY • 86
SOUNDS LIKE FUN
INITIAL SOUND /h/ • 87
PEOPLE WHO CARE
HEALTHY CHOICES • 88
GAMES AND CHALLENGES
ROULETTE GAME • 89
LET'S READ IMAGES!
IMAGES FOR GAMES • 90

FOLLOW-UP • 92
WORKBOOK • 96
PROJECTS • 112
CLASSROOM LANGUAGE • 120
GLOSSARY • 123
PRESS OUTS • 129
STICKERS • 137

NINE 9

WELCOME

HELLO, COME IN!

1 LOOK AND MATCH.

STUDENTS

GIRL

TEACHER

BOY

2 🎧 02 LISTEN AND SAY.

3 🎧 03 LISTEN, POINT AND SAY. 😊

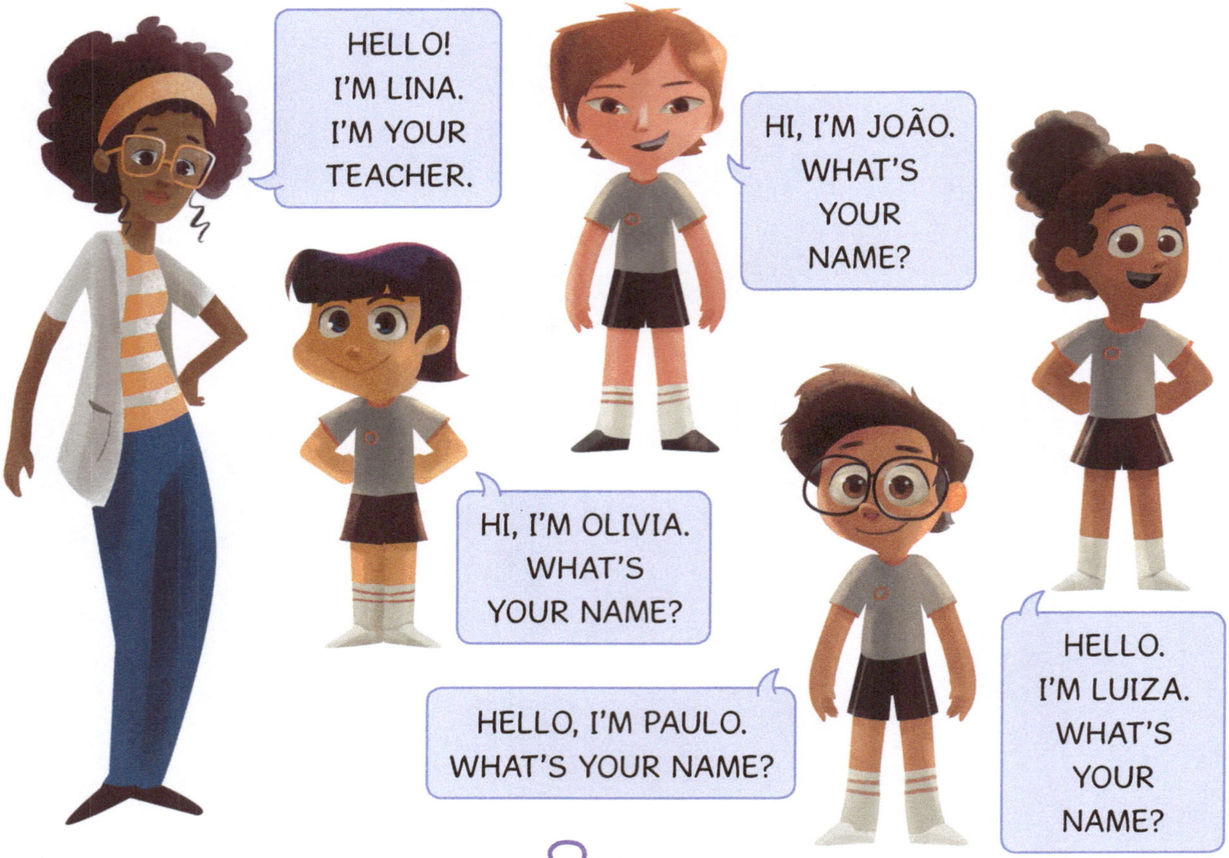

4 DRAW, WRITE AND SAY. 😊

HELLO! I'M _____.

5  LISTEN AND SING.

WHAT'S YOUR NAME?

HI, I'M LINA. WHAT'S YOUR NAME?
I'M OLIVIA. IT'S GOOD TO MEET YOU.

HI, I'M PAULO. WHAT'S YOUR NAME?
I'M LUIZA. IT'S GOOD TO MEET YOU.

HI, I'M ANA. WHAT'S YOUR NAME?
I'M FELIPE. IT'S GOOD TO MEET YOU.

HI, I'M GABI. WHAT'S YOUR NAME?
I'M BERNARDO. IT'S GOOD TO MEET YOU.

THIRTEEN 13

6 LOOK AND LISTEN.

您好，我是华。

مرحبا. انا اسمي علي.

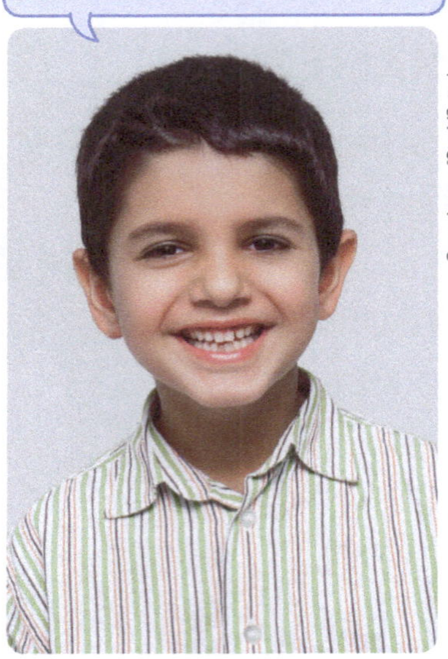

में आर्यन हु.

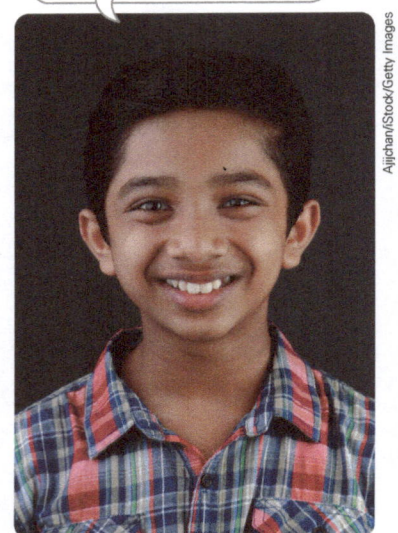

7 LOOK, LISTEN AND SAY.

HI, I'M HUA.

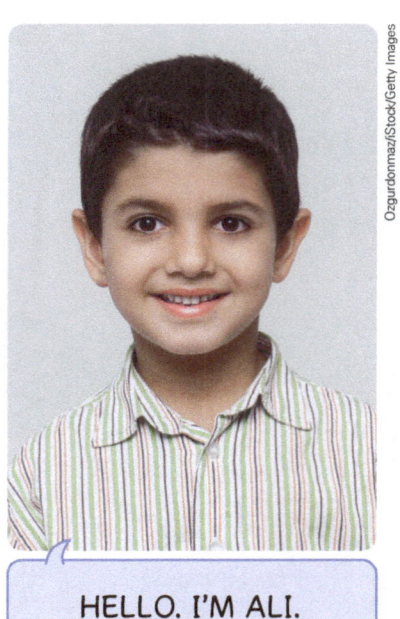

HELLO. I'M ALI.

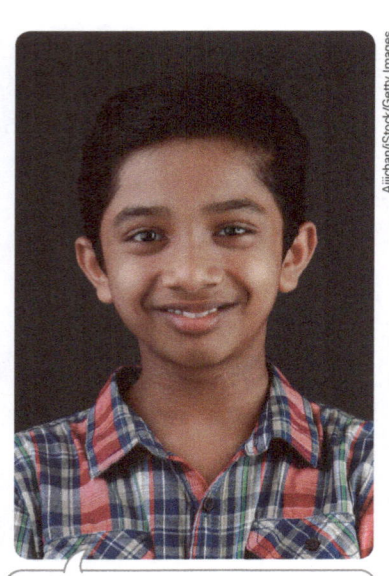

HI! I'M ARYAN.

8 07 LISTEN, STICK AND SAY.

PLAYGROUND TABLET BANANA GAME

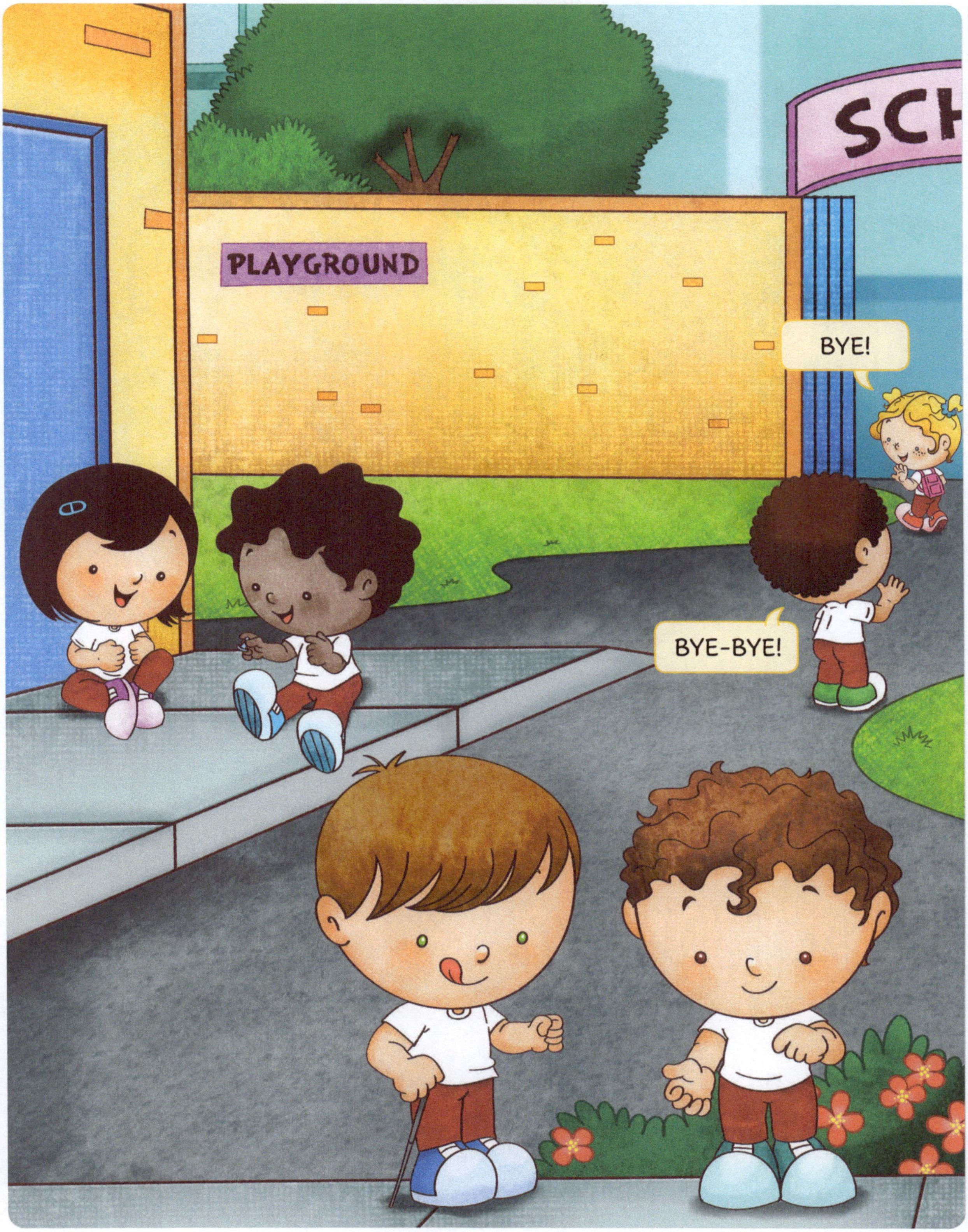

Alexandre Matos/ID/BR

LANGUAGE CORNER

3 09 LISTEN AND STICK.

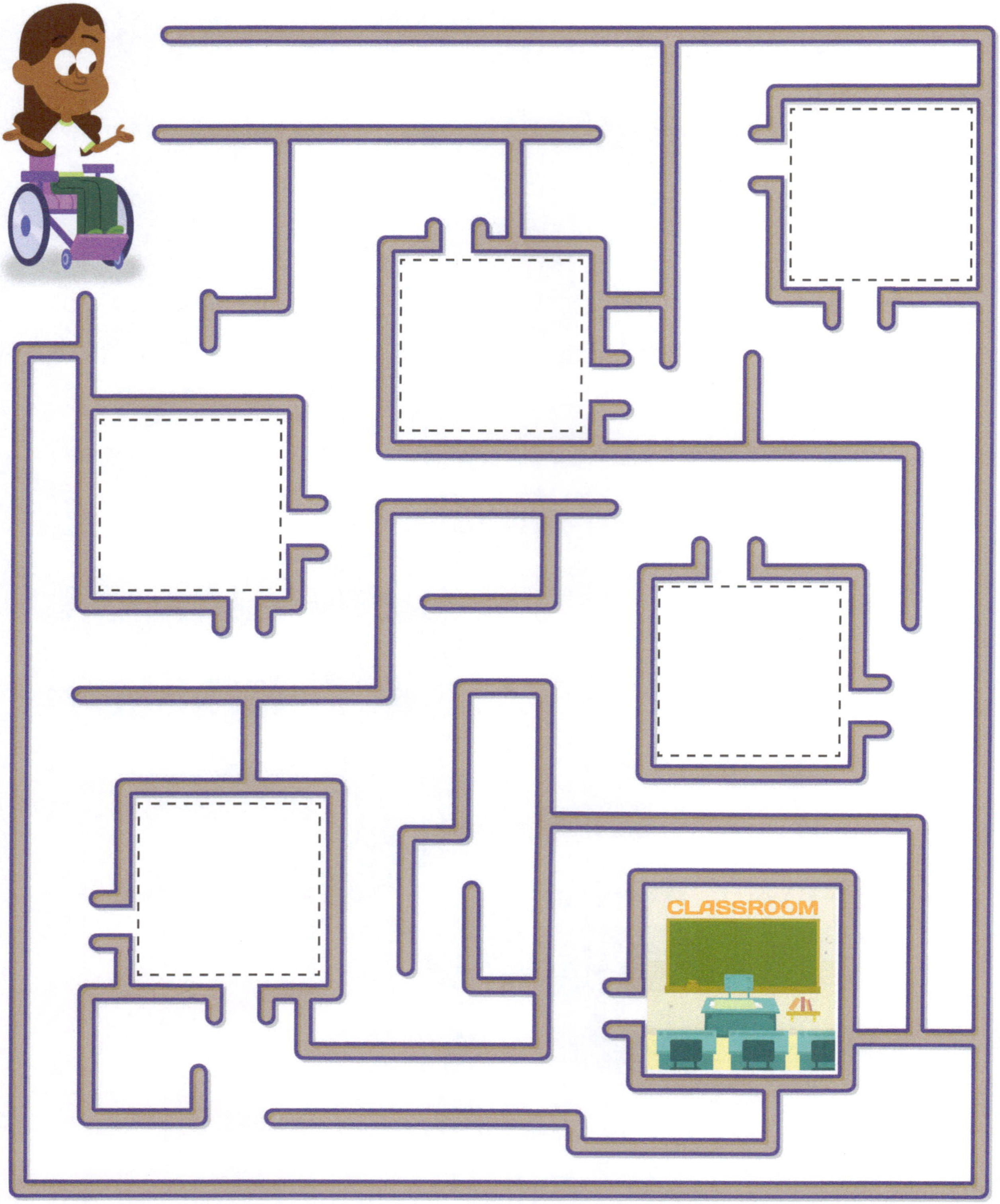

Illustrations: Chris Borges/ID/BR

4 10 MATCH AND LISTEN.

CONTEÚDO NA VERSÃO DIGITAL

LEFT		RIGHT

Illustrations: Chris Borges/ID/BR

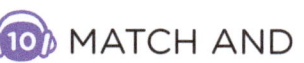

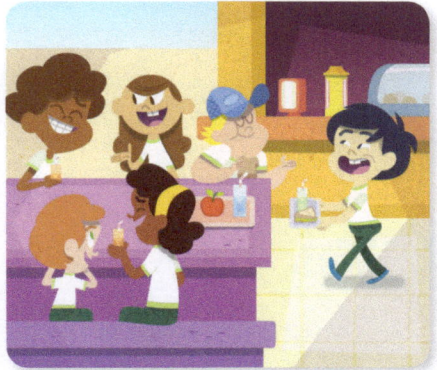

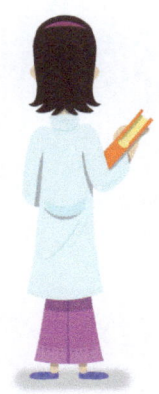

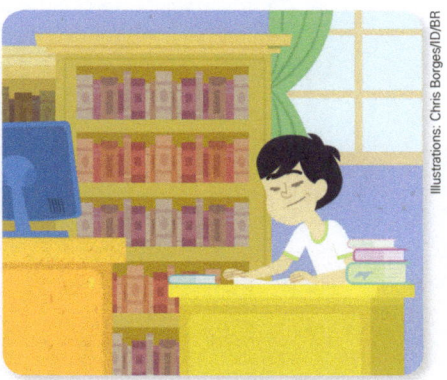

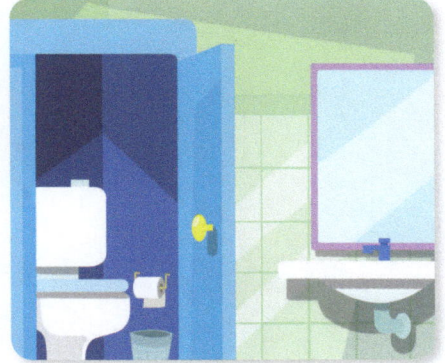

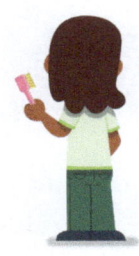

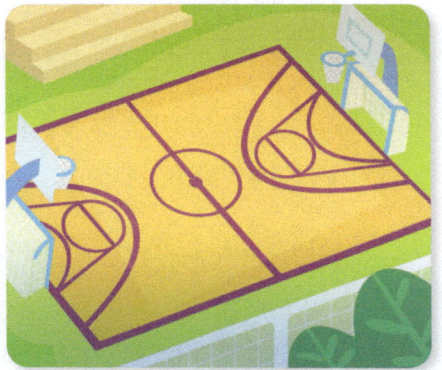

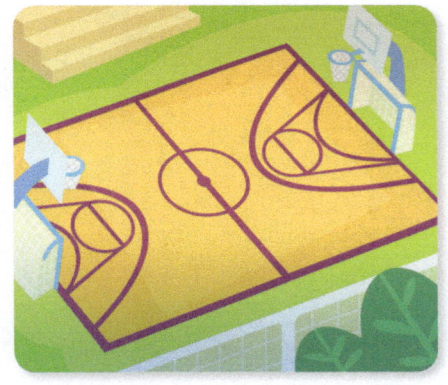

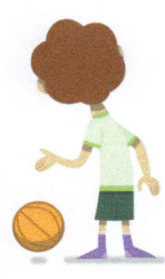

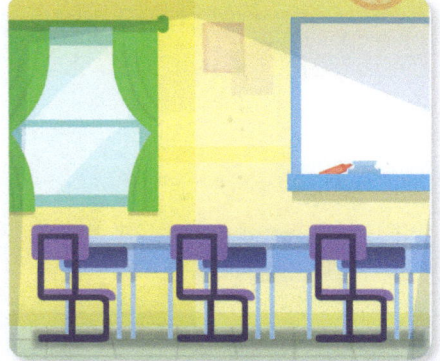

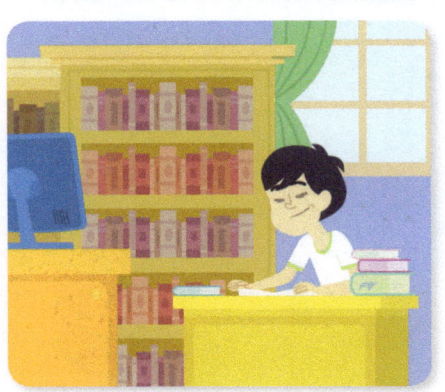

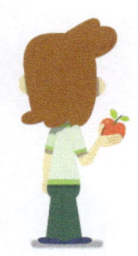

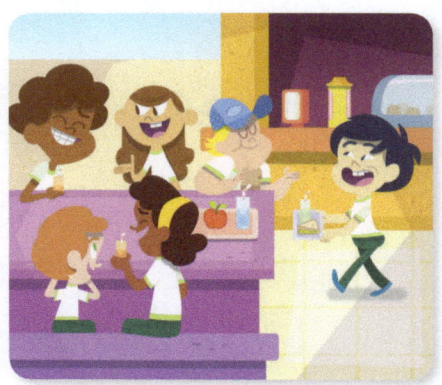

SING ALONG

5 SING AND ACT OUT.

WELCOME TO SCHOOL

WELCOME, WELCOME,
WELCOME TO SCHOOL (X2)

HO! THIS IS THE GYM
WELCOME TO SCHOOL (X2)

SHH! THIS IS THE LIBRARY
WELCOME TO SCHOOL (X2)

PHEW! THIS IS THE RESTROOM
WELCOME TO SCHOOL (X2)

HURRAY! THIS IS THE PLAYGROUND
WELCOME TO SCHOOL (X2)

OKAY! THIS IS THE CLASSROOM
WELCOME TO SCHOOL (X2)

SOUNDS LIKE FUN

  LISTEN, REPEAT AND CIRCLE.

TWENTY-ONE 21

PEOPLE WHO CARE

CARE AND KINDNESS

7 LOOK, CROSS OUT AND CIRCLE.

DON'T BE CARELESS   SHARE THINGS   PLAY TOGETHER

8 CUT AND GLUE.

GAMES AND CHALLENGES

9 FIND THE PATH.

WORKBOOK
GO TO PAGE **96**.

TWENTY-THREE **23**

UNIT 2 SCHOOL STUFF

1. LOOK, LISTEN AND SAY.

LOOK AT MY NEW STUFF! MY SCHOOL BAG, A RULER, CRAYONS, A PEN...

...A SHARPENER, PENCILS, AN ERASER AND A NOTEBOOK.

LANGUAGE CORNER

2   LISTEN AND CHECK.

WHAT'S THIS?

A
IT'S A PENCIL.   IT'S A BOOK.

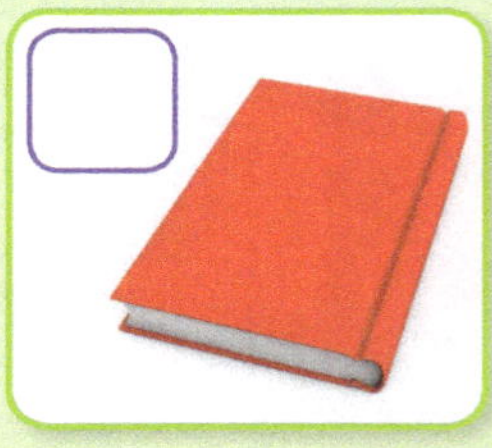

B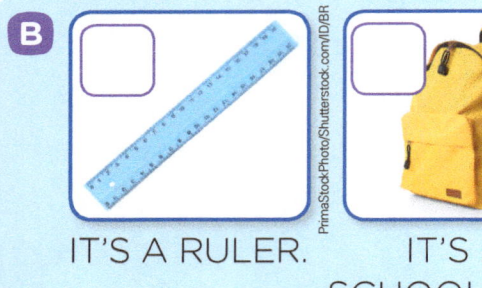
IT'S A RULER.   IT'S A SCHOOL BAG.

C
IT'S A CRAYON.   IT'S AN ERASER.

D
IT'S A PEN.   IT'S A SHARPENER.

3 TOUCH AND SAY.

WHAT'S THIS?   IT'S A RULER.

26 TWENTY-SIX

LISTEN, STICK AND SAY.

 ONE

 TWO

 THREE

 FOUR

 FIVE

SING ALONG

5 CROSS OUT AND SING. 🎵

WHAT'S THIS?

WHAT'S THIS?

WHAT'S THIS? (X8)

WHAT'S THIS?
IT'S A PENCIL
WHAT'S THIS?
IT'S A CRAYON
WHAT'S THIS?
IT'S A SNAKE
OOOOH, YUCKY!

WHAT'S THIS? (X8)

WHAT'S THIS?
IT'S A NOTEBOOK
WHAT'S THIS?
IT'S AN ERASER
WHAT'S THIS?
IT'S A SPIDER
OOOOH, YUCKY!

WHAT'S THIS? (X8)

WHAT'S THIS?
IT'S A PEN
WHAT'S THIS?
IT'S A RULER
WHAT'S THIS?
IT'S A WORM
OOOOH, YUCKY!

PENCIL

CRAYON

NOTEBOOK

ERASER

SPIDER

RULER

PEN

SNAKE

WORM

DREAM ENGLISH KIDS. *WHAT'S THIS?* AVAILABLE AT https://www.dreamenglish.com/starkids/whatsthis. ACCESSED ON FEBRUARY 4, 2021.

28 TWENTY-EIGHT

SOUNDS LIKE FUN

  LISTEN, SAY AND CIRCLE.

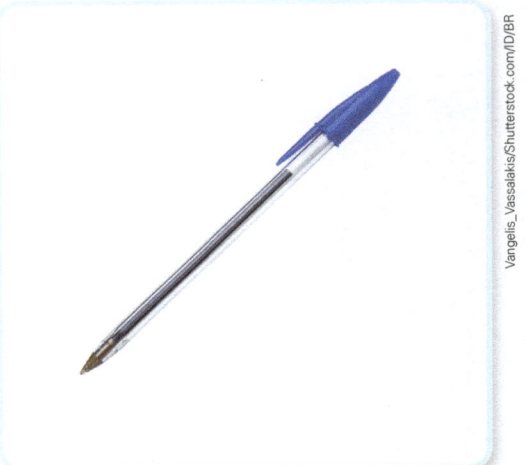

PEOPLE WHO CARE

ORGANIZING YOURSELF

 7 CROSS OUT THE DIFFERENCES AND COLOR.

GAMES AND CHALLENGES

SCAVENGER HUNT

8 FIND AND COLOR.

CRAYONS

SPIDER

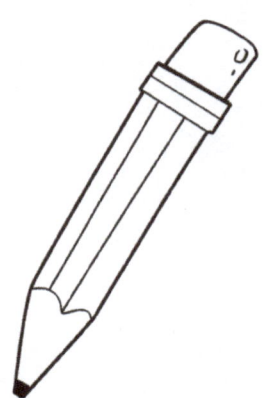

PENCIL

SNAKE

BOOK

WORM

WORKBOOK
GO TO PAGE **98**.

THIRTY-ONE 31

PEOPLE AND PLACES

GOING TO SCHOOL

1 LOOK AT THE PICTURES.

IN THE USA, MOST KIDS GO TO SCHOOL BY BUS.

IN JAPAN, YOUNG KIDS TAKE THE SUBWAY TO GO TO SCHOOL.

IN SOME VILLAGES FROM PHILLIPPINES, KIDS GO TO SCHOOL BY BOAT.

IN INDIA, MANY KIDS WALK TO SCHOOL.

IN COPENHAGEN, DENMARK, IT IS COMMON TO SEE PARENTS TAKING THE KIDS TO SCHOOL BY BIKE.

SOURCES: https://sn4.scholastic.com/issues/2019-20/090219/how-do-you-get-to-school.html; https://www.easyvoyage.co.uk/travel-headlines/how-children-get-to-school-7-countries-83832. ACCESSED ON FEBRUARY 4, 2021.

2 DRAW HOW YOU GO TO SCHOOL.

35

LANGUAGE CORNER

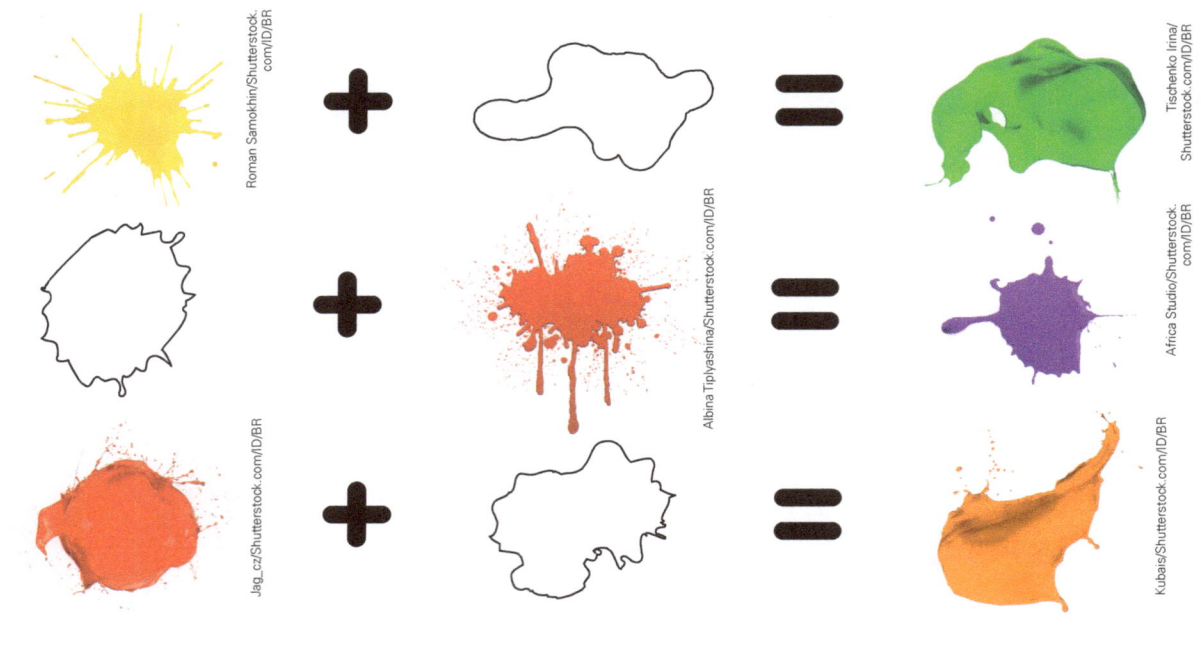

3 🎧 19 COLOR, LISTEN AND SAY. 😊

4 COLOR BY NUMBER.

1. RED   2. YELLOW   3. BLUE   4. ORANGE   5. GREEN OR PURPLE

36 THIRTY-SIX

5 STICK AND ACT OUT.

WHAT'S THIS?

IT'S MY BLUE SCHOOL BAG.

WHAT'S THIS?

OH! A PURPLE SUN!

IT'S A YELLOW APPLE.

SING ALONG

6 🎧 20 SING AND GLUE. 🎵

WHAT COLOR IS THE SKY?

WHAT COLOR IS THE SKY?
IT'S **BLUE**
IT'S **BLUE**
IT'S **BLUE**
THE SKY IS **BLUE**
THE SKY IS **BLUE**

WHAT COLOR IS THE SUN?
IT'S **YELLOW**
IT'S **YELLOW**
IT'S **YELLOW**
THE SUN IS **YELLOW**
THE SKY IS **BLUE**

WHAT COLOR IS THE GRASS?
IT'S **GREEN**
IT'S **GREEN**
IT'S **GREEN**
THE GRASS IS **GREEN**
THE SUN IS **YELLOW**
THE SKY IS **BLUE**

WHAT COLOR IS AN APPLE?
IT'S **RED**
IT'S **RED**
IT'S **RED**
AN APPLE IS **RED**
THE GRASS IS **GREEN**
THE SUN IS **YELLOW**
THE SKY IS **BLUE**
THE SKY IS **BLUE**

WRIGHT CHRISTOPHER. *WHAT COLOR IS THE SKY?*
AVAILABLE AT https://www.youtube.com/watch?v=7jW1E8f2qO4.
ACCESSED ON FEBRUARY 4, 2021.

SOUNDS LIKE FUN

7 🎧 21 **LISTEN AND SAY.** 💬

HI, RACHEL!

HELLO, WILLIAM.

8 🎧 22 **LISTEN, SAY AND CIRCLE.** 💬

THIRTY-NINE **39**

PEOPLE WHO CARE

ATTENTION

9 🎧 23 LISTEN AND POINT.

> RED ON TOP, GREEN BELOW.
> RED SAYS STOP!, GREEN SAYS GO!
> YELLOW SAYS WAIT EVEN IF YOU'RE LATE.

10 LOOK AND COLOR.

GAMES AND CHALLENGES

11 PLAY.

START

MISS A TURN

MOVE AHEAD 3

MOVE TO YELLOW

GO BACK 2

MOVE TO PURPLE

WORKBOOK GO TO PAGE **100**.

GO BACK 5

MISS A TURN

FINISH

UNIT 4
THE PLAYGROUND

1 🎧 24 LISTEN, POINT AND SAY.

I LOVE THE SLIDE!

SLIDE DOWN!

SWINGS!
LET'S PLAY!
MONKEY BARS
ARE FUN.
I LOVE TO PLAY IN
THE PLAYGROUND!
Sergiy Kuzmin/Shutterstock.com/ID/BR
Bruna Assis Brasil/ID/BR

LANGUAGE CORNER

2 MATCH AND SAY.

A SWING. LET'S PLAY!

A TRAMPOLINE. LET'S PLAY!

A SLIDE. LET'S PLAY!

A BALL. LET'S PLAY!

MONKEY BARS. LET'S PLAY!

A SEESAW. LET'S PLAY!

3 🎧 **LISTEN AND COLOR.**

A

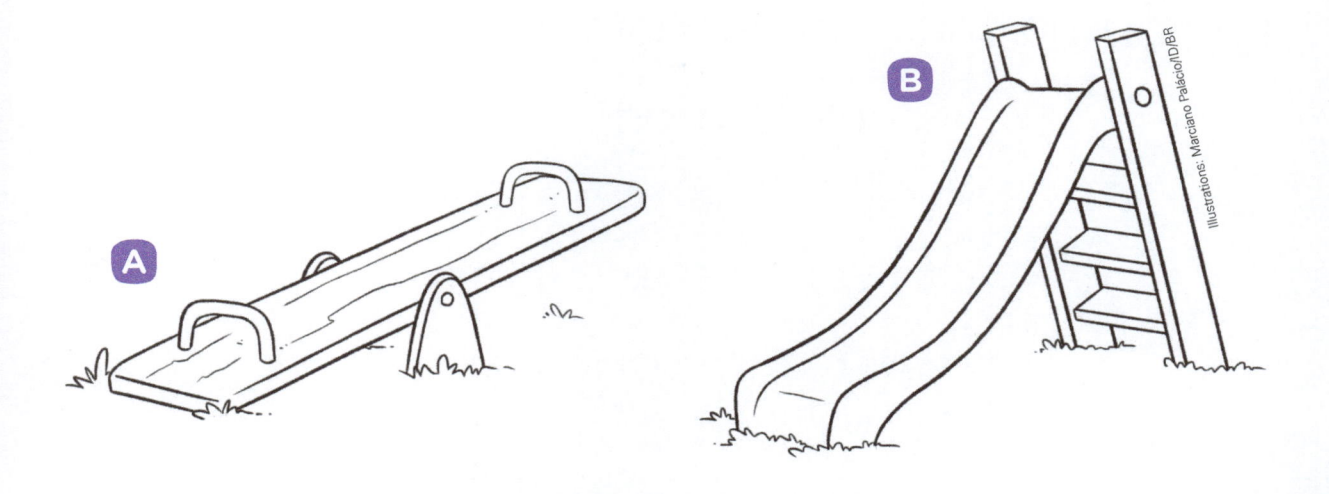

B

C

D

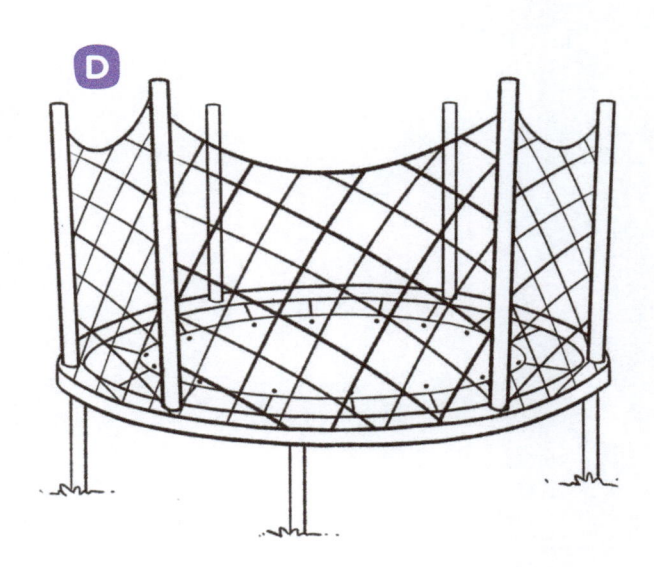

E

FORTY-FIVE **45**

SING ALONG

4 🎧26 SING, DANCE AND MAKE A SOUND.

LET'S PLAY!

SLIDES ARE FUN AND SO ARE MONKEY BARS
LET'S PLAY!
UP AND DOWN I GO ON THE SEESAW
LET'S PLAY!
I LOVE THE SWING, I LOVE THE TRAMPOLINE
LET'S PLAY!

46 FORTY-SIX

SOUNDS LIKE FUN

5 🎧 **27** LISTEN, CIRCLE AND STICK.

PEOPLE WHO CARE

COOPERATION

6 LOOK AND STICK.

DON'T ARGUE.

BE KIND.

DON'T BREAK THINGS.

PLAY TOGETHER.

48 FORTY-EIGHT

GAMES AND CHALLENGES

7 🎧 **28** LISTEN, FIND AND CIRCLE.

WORKBOOK
GO TO PAGE **102**.

FORTY-NINE 49

LET'S READ IMAGES!

COLORS IN NATURE

1 LOOK AND WRITE.

A

B

C

D

2 LOOK AND MATCH.

- [ ] SUMMER
- [ ] FALL / AUTUMN
- [ ] WINTER
- [ ] SPRING

50 FIFTY

3 DRAW AND COLOR.

FOLLOW-UP

1 🎧 29 LISTEN AND NUMBER.

☐ THIS IS THE CAFETERIA. 😊 😐

☐ THIS IS THE RESTROOM. 😊 😐

☐ THIS IS THE LIBRARY. 😊 😐

☐ THIS IS THE CLASSROOM. 😊 😐

☐ THIS IS THE GYM. 😊 😐

HOW MANY 😊? ☐

52 FIFTY-TWO

2 🎧 30 LISTEN AND CIRCLE.

HOW MANY 😊 ?

FIFTY-THREE 53

3 LOOK AND CHECK.

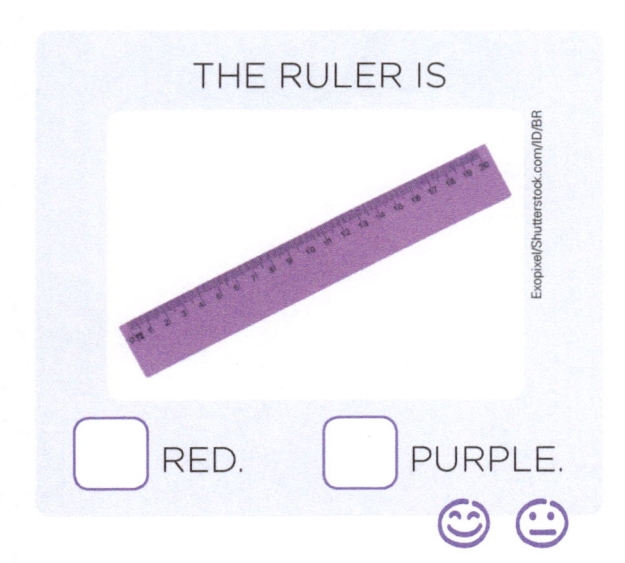

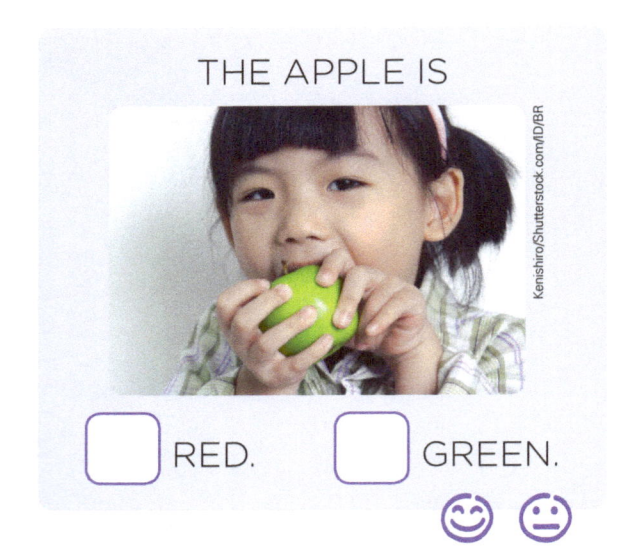

THE CRAYON IS
☐ ORANGE. ☐ BLUE.
😊 😐

THE APPLE IS
☐ RED. ☐ GREEN.
😊 😐

THE BOOK IS
☐ BLUE. ☐ RED.
😊 😐

THE SUN IS
☐ GREEN. ☐ YELLOW.
😊 😐

THE RULER IS
☐ RED. ☐ PURPLE.
😊 😐

HOW MANY 😊? ☐

4 MATCH AND SAY.

HOW MANY 😊?

GENERAL SELF-ASSESSMENT - UNITS 1-4

I CAN IMPROVE.    GOOD!    GREAT!

UNIT 5
SHAPES AND FUN

1 🎧 31 LOOK, LISTEN AND FIND.

I CAN SEE A CIRCLE.

OH! A HULA HOOP.

A DOMINO!

I CAN SEE A RECTANGLE.

TOY LIBRARY

THREE SIDES!

A SQUARE!

HMM! FOUR SIDES. THEY ARE THE SAME...

HEY YOU, LET'S FIND A STAR.

YES! I CAN MAKE A TRIANGLE, TOO.

LANGUAGE CORNER

2 🎧 32 LISTEN, FIND AND COLOR.

3 🎧 33 LISTEN, STICK AND SAY.

NUMBERS

6 SIX

7 SEVEN

8 EIGHT

9 NINE

10 TEN

FIFTY-NINE 59

SING ALONG

4 🎧 **34** SING AND SHOW.

SHAPES SONG

A CIRCLE
A TRIANGLE   CHORUS (X2)
A SQUARE
A HEART

CAN YOU SEE A CIRCLE?
YES, I CAN
CAN YOU SEE A CIRCLE?
YES, I CAN
CAN YOU SEE A TRIANGLE?
YES, I CAN
CAN YOU SEE A TRIANGLE?
YES, I CAN

CHORUS

CAN YOU SEE A SQUARE?
YES, I CAN
CAN YOU SEE A SQUARE?
YES, I CAN
CAN YOU SEE A HEART?
YES, I CAN
CAN YOU SEE A HEART?
YES, I CAN

CHORUS

CAN YOU MAKE A...?

CAN YOU TOUCH A...?

DREAM ENGLISH KIDS. *SHAPES SONG*. AVAILABLE AT https://www.youtube.com/watch?v=g2jdZ46nK-M. ACCESSED ON FEBRUARY 5, 2021.

SOUNDS LIKE FUN

5 🎧 35 **LISTEN, REPEAT AND COMPLETE.**

SHH!

☐☐APES

☐☐ARPENER

☐☐ARE

☐☐ORTS

☐☐AMPOO

SIXTY-ONE 61

PEOPLE WHO CARE

ATTENTION AND RESPECT

6 CIRCLE AND CROSS OUT.

62 SIXTY-TWO

GAMES AND CHALLENGES

7 PLAY.

WORKBOOK
GO TO PAGE **104**.

UNIT 6 MY BODY

1 🎧 36 LOOK, LISTEN AND SAY.

LOOK AT MY ARMS.

LOOK! MY FEET!

65

LANGUAGE CORNER

MY BODY

2 LOOK, STICK AND SAY.

EARS

NOSE

EYES

MOUTH

3 🎧 37 MATCH AND LISTEN.

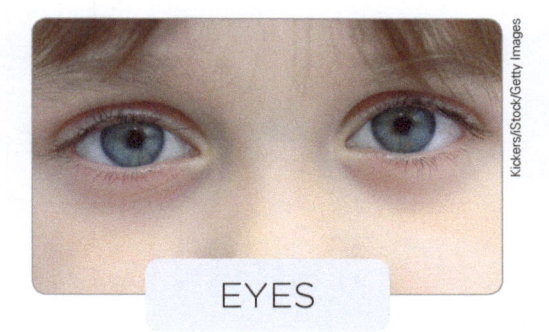

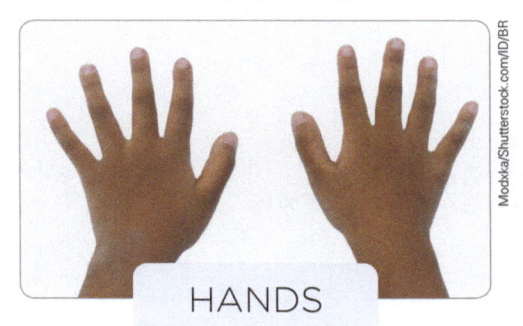

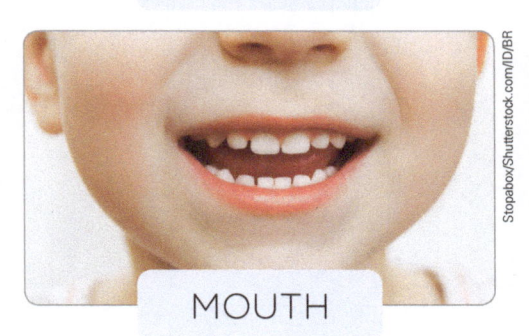

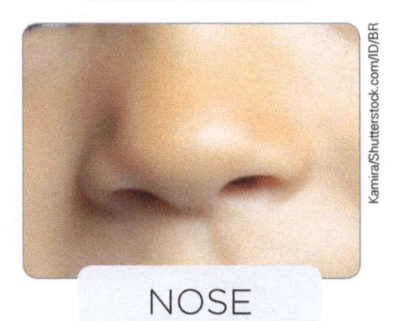

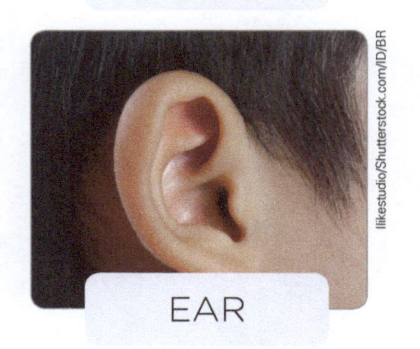

SMELL

EYES

HEARING

HANDS

SIGHT

MOUTH

TOUCH

NOSE

TASTE

EAR

SIXTY-SEVEN **67**

SING ALONG

4 🎧 38 SING AND DANCE. 🎵

THE HOKEY COKEY

YOU PUT YOUR LEFT ARM IN,
YOUR LEFT ARM OUT
IN, OUT, IN, OUT, YOU SHAKE IT ALL ABOUT
YOU DO THE HOKEY COKEY AND YOU TURN AROUND
THAT'S WHAT IT'S ALL ABOUT
WHOA-O THE HOKEY COKEY (X3)
KNEES BENT, ARMS STRETCHED
RAH! RAH! RAH!

YOU PUT YOUR RIGHT ARM IN,
YOUR RIGHT ARM OUT
IN, OUT, IN, OUT, YOU SHAKE IT ALL ABOUT
YOU DO THE HOKEY COKEY AND YOU TURN AROUND
THAT'S WHAT IT'S ALL ABOUT
WHOA-O THE HOKEY COKEY (X3)
KNEES BENT, ARMS STRETCHED
RAH! RAH! RAH!

YOU PUT YOUR LEFT LEG IN,
YOUR LEFT LEG OUT
IN, OUT, IN, OUT, YOU SHAKE IT ALL ABOUT
YOU DO THE HOKEY COKEY AND YOU TURN AROUND
THAT'S WHAT IT'S ALL ABOUT

WHOA-O THE HOKEY COKEY (X3)
KNEES BENT, ARMS STRETCHED
RAH! RAH! RAH!

YOU PUT YOUR RIGHT LEG IN,
YOUR RIGHT LEG OUT
IN, OUT, IN, OUT, YOU SHAKE IT ALL ABOUT
YOU DO THE HOKEY COKEY AND YOU TURN AROUND
THAT'S WHAT IT'S ALL ABOUT
WHOA-O THE HOKEY COKEY (X3)
KNEES BENT, ARMS STRETCHED
RAH! RAH! RAH!

YOU PUT YOUR WHOLE SELF IN,
YOUR WHOLE SELF OUT
IN, OUT, IN, OUT, YOU SHAKE IT ALL ABOUT
YOU DO THE HOKEY COKEY AND YOU TURN AROUND
THAT'S WHAT IT'S ALL ABOUT
WHOA-O THE HOKEY COKEY (X3)
KNEES BENT, ARMS STRETCHED
RAH! RAH! RAH!

PUBLIC DOMAIN.

SOUNDS LIKE FUN

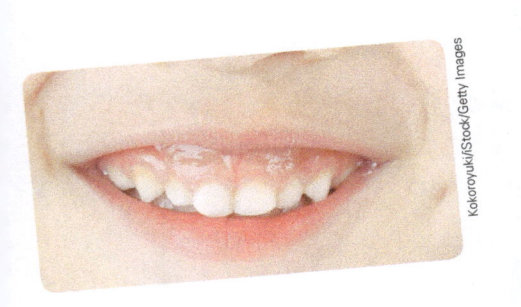

5 🎧 39 LISTEN, SAY AND CIRCLE.

6 COLOR AND COMPLETE.

☐ OOK ☐ ALL ☐ ODY

SIXTY-NINE 69

PEOPLE WHO CARE

HEALTHY HABITS

7 NUMBER THE PICTURES.

WASH YOUR HANDS

DRY YOUR HANDS

EAT LUNCH

PLAY WITH THE DOG

GAMES AND CHALLENGES

8 PLAY.

WORKBOOK GO TO PAGE **106**.

PEOPLE AND PLACES

FLAGS, SHAPES AND COLORS

1 READ AND CHECK.

A. THIS FLAG IS FROM JAPAN.

SHAPES
- [ ] CIRCLE
- [ ] SQUARE
- [ ] TRIANGLE
- [ ] STAR

COLORS
- [ ] WHITE
- [ ] RED
- [ ] GREEN
- [ ] BLUE
- [ ] YELLOW

B. THIS FLAG IS FROM THE UNITED STATES OF AMERICA.

SHAPES
- [ ] CIRCLE
- [ ] SQUARE
- [ ] RHOMBUS
- [ ] STAR

COLORS
- [ ] WHITE
- [ ] RED
- [ ] GREEN
- [ ] BLUE
- [ ] YELLOW

C. THIS FLAG IS FROM ITALY.

SHAPES
- ☐ CIRCLE
- ☐ SQUARE
- ☐ TRIANGLE
- ☐ STAR

COLORS
- ☐ WHITE
- ☐ RED
- ☐ GREEN
- ☐ BLUE
- ☐ YELLOW

D. THIS FLAG IS FROM BRAZIL.

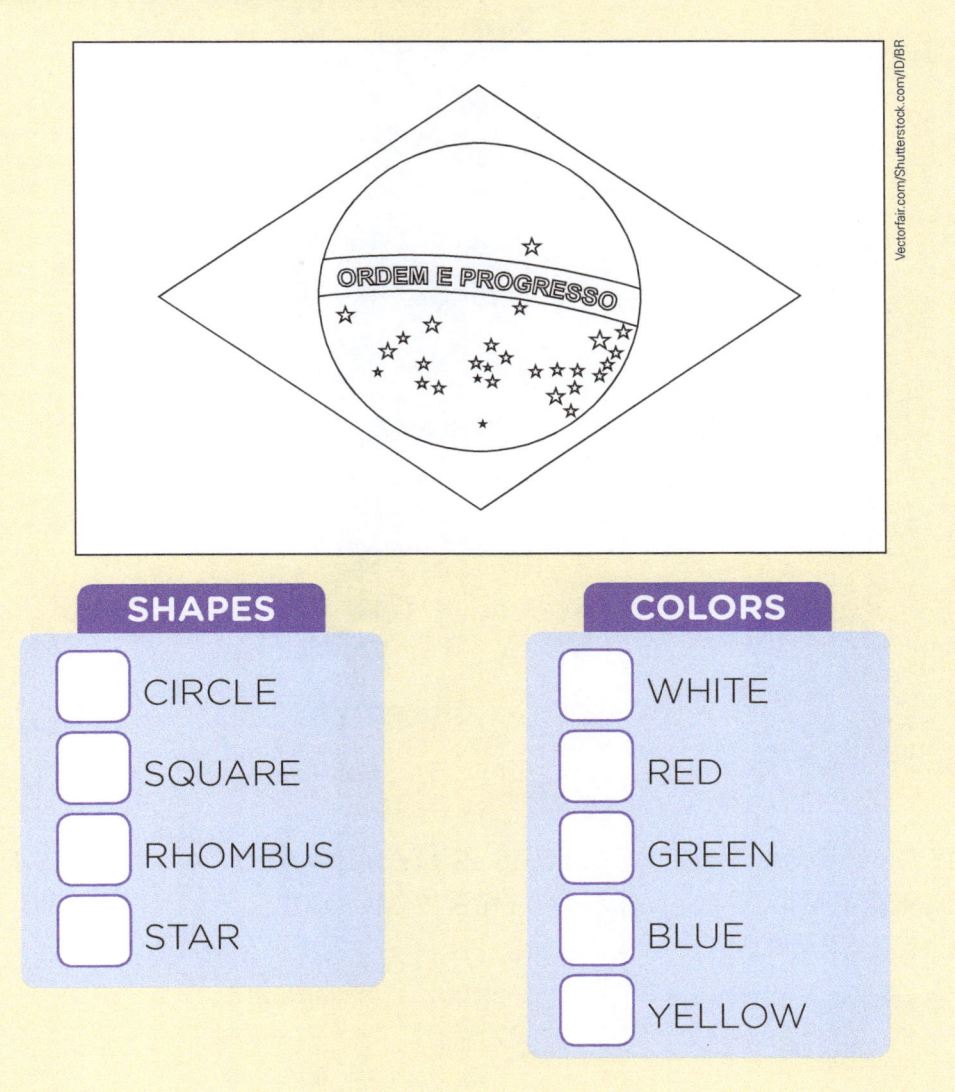

SHAPES
- ☐ CIRCLE
- ☐ SQUARE
- ☐ RHOMBUS
- ☐ STAR

COLORS
- ☐ WHITE
- ☐ RED
- ☐ GREEN
- ☐ BLUE
- ☐ YELLOW

2 COLOR.

UNIT 7
MY FAMILY

1 🎧 40 LOOK, LISTEN AND SAY.

HI. LOOK AT MY FAMILY TREE.

THIS IS MY GRANDMA, THIS IS MY GRANDPA AND THIS IS MY OTHER GRANDMA.

THIS IS MY MOM AND THIS IS MY DAD.

THIS IS MY SISTER AND THIS IS ME!

THIS IS MY FAMILY TREE!

THIS IS MY GRANDPA AND THIS IS MY GRANDMA.

THIS IS MY MOM, THIS IS MY BROTHER AND THIS IS ME.

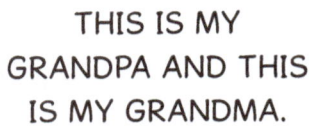

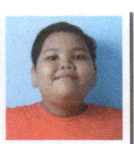

I LOVE MY FAMILY!

75

LANGUAGE CORNER

2 🎧 41 LISTEN AND STICK.

ME

3 DRAW AND SAY.

THIS IS MY FAMILY.

76 SEVENTY-SIX

4 COMPLETE.

SISTER   GRANDPA   MOM   BROTHER   DAD   GRANDMA

```
            G
            R
        F A M I L Y
            N   S
            D   I
          A     S
            P   T
    B       A   E
  G R A N D M A R
    O       M
    T
    H
    E
    R
```

SING ALONG

5 🎧 42 SING AND SHOW. 🎴 🎵

THE FINGER FAMILY

DADDY FINGER, DADDY FINGER,
WHERE ARE YOU?
HERE I AM, HERE I AM
HOW DO YOU DO?

MOMMY FINGER, MOMMY FINGER,
WHERE ARE YOU?
HERE I AM, HERE I AM
HOW DO YOU DO?

BROTHER FINGER, BROTHER FINGER,
WHERE ARE YOU?
HERE I AM, HERE I AM
HOW DO YOU DO?

SISTER FINGER, SISTER FINGER,
WHERE ARE YOU?
HERE I AM, HERE I AM
HOW DO YOU DO?

BABY FINGER, BABY FINGER,
WHERE ARE YOU?
HERE I AM, HERE I AM
HOW DO YOU DO?

PUBLIC DOMAIN.

SOUNDS LIKE FUN

6 🎧43 COMPLETE, LISTEN AND SAY. 💬

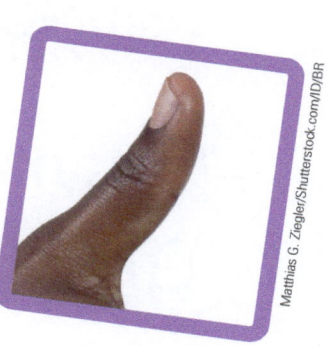

☐ AMILY

☐ IVE   ☐ OUR   ☐ INGER

7 🎧44 LISTEN AND REPEAT. 💬

FINN AND FIONA'S FAMILY IS FUN!

SEVENTY-NINE

PEOPLE WHO CARE

LOVE AND RESPECT

8 READ AND DRAW ☺ OR ☹.

I LOVE YOU GRANDMA

YOU ARE NOT MY BROTHER ANYMORE

I'M SORRY! YOU ARE A SUPER SISTER

I MISS YOU DAD

GAMES AND CHALLENGES

9 PLAY.

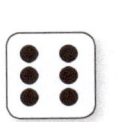

- ⚀ GRANDPA 
- ⚁ GRANDMA 
- ⚂ DAD 
- ⚃ MOM 
- ⚄ SISTER 
- ⚅ BABY BROTHER

WORKBOOK
GO TO PAGE **108**.

EIGHTY-ONE 81

UNIT 8 BREAK TIME

1 🎧45 LISTEN, POINT AND SAY.

MENU
- COOKIES ... $2
- BANANA ... $1
- SANDWICH ... $5
- ORANGE JUICE ... $3
- WATER ... $1

WATER, PLEASE.

I LOVE ORANGE JUICE!

LET'S PLAY HOPSCOTCH!

WE LOVE TO PLAY MARBLES!

MY FAVORITE GAME IS HIDE AND SEEK.

WHAT'S YOUR FAVORITE GAME?

TIC-TAC-TOE IS FUN!

2 CHOOSE A FRIEND AND PLAY TIC-TAC-TOE.

83

LANGUAGE CORNER

3 DRAW, COMPLETE AND SAY.

I LOVE B[A]N[A]N[A]S.

WE LOVE [O]R[A]NG[E] JUICE.

WE LOVE C[O][O]K[IE]S.

I LOVE TO PLAY H[O]PSC[O]TCH.

WE LOVE TO PLAY T[I]C-T[A]C-T[O]E.

84 EIGHTY-FOUR

4 🎧 **LISTEN AND NUMBER.**

EIGHTY-FIVE 85

SING ALONG

5 **47** LISTEN, MATCH AND SING. 🎵

LET'S PLAY

LET'S PLAY, LET'S PLAY
WE LOVE HOPSCOTCH
LET'S PLAY, LET'S PLAY
WE LOVE HOPSCOTCH SO

JUMP, JUMP, JUMP
ONE LEG, TWO LEGS
JUMP, JUMP, JUMP
ONE LEG, TWO LEGS SO

LET'S PLAY, LET'S PLAY
WE LOVE HIDE AND SEEK
LET'S PLAY, LET'S PLAY
WE LOVE HIDE AND SEEK SO

COUNT TO TEN
RUN AND HIDE
COUNT TO TEN
RUN AND HIDE, SO

LET'S PLAY, LET'S PLAY
WE LOVE TIC-TAC-TOE
LET'S PLAY, LET'S PLAY
WE LOVE TIC-TAC-TOE SO

I AM X
YOU ARE O
I AM X
YOU ARE O, SO

LET'S PLAY, LET'S PLAY
WE LOVE MARBLES
LET'S PLAY, LET'S PLAY
WE LOVE MARBLES SO

ONE GREEN MARBLE
FOUR GREEN MARBLES
ONE GREEN MARBLE
FOUR GREEN MARBLES, SO

LET'S PLAY, LET'S PLAY
WE LOVE EVERY GAME
LET'S PLAY, LET'S PLAY
WE LOVE EVERY GAME SO

SOUNDS LIKE FUN

6 🎧 **48** LISTEN, SAY AND CIRCLE.

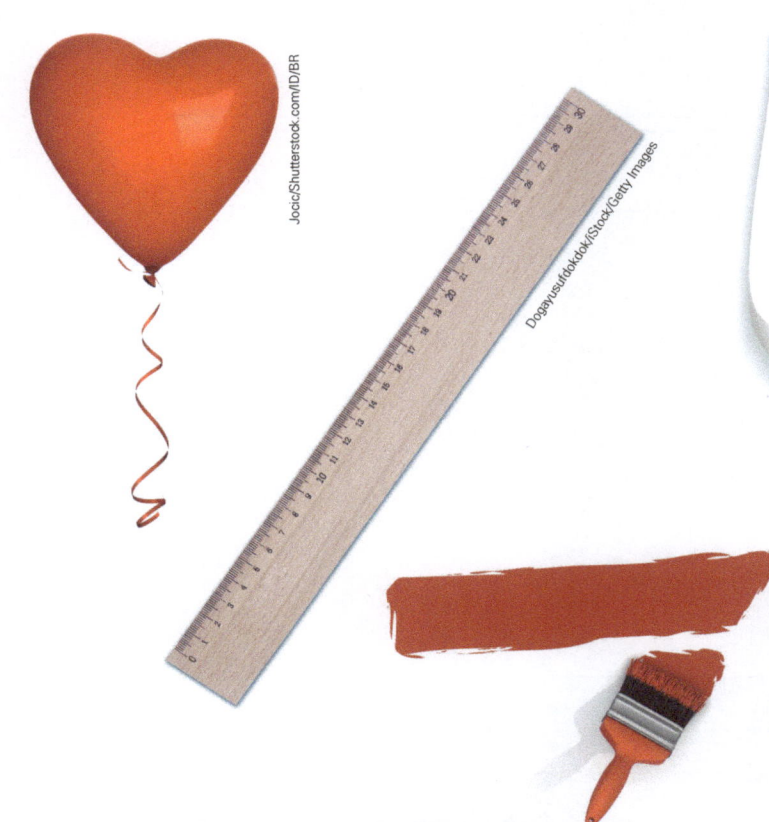

EIGHTY-SEVEN 87

PEOPLE WHO CARE

HEALTHY CHOICES

7 LOOK AND STICK.

88 EIGHTY-EIGHT

GAMES AND CHALLENGES

8 PLAY.

EIGHTY-NINE 89

WORKBOOK
GO TO PAGE **110**.

LET'S READ IMAGES!

IMAGES FOR GAMES

1 LOOK AND COLOR.

2. READ AND NUMBER.

☐ PLAY AGAIN   ☐ MISS A TURN

☐ MOVE FORWARD   ☐ MOVE BACK

3. PLAY.

4. DRAW AND COLOR.

5. PLAY.

FOLLOW-UP

1 FIND, COLOR AND COUNT.

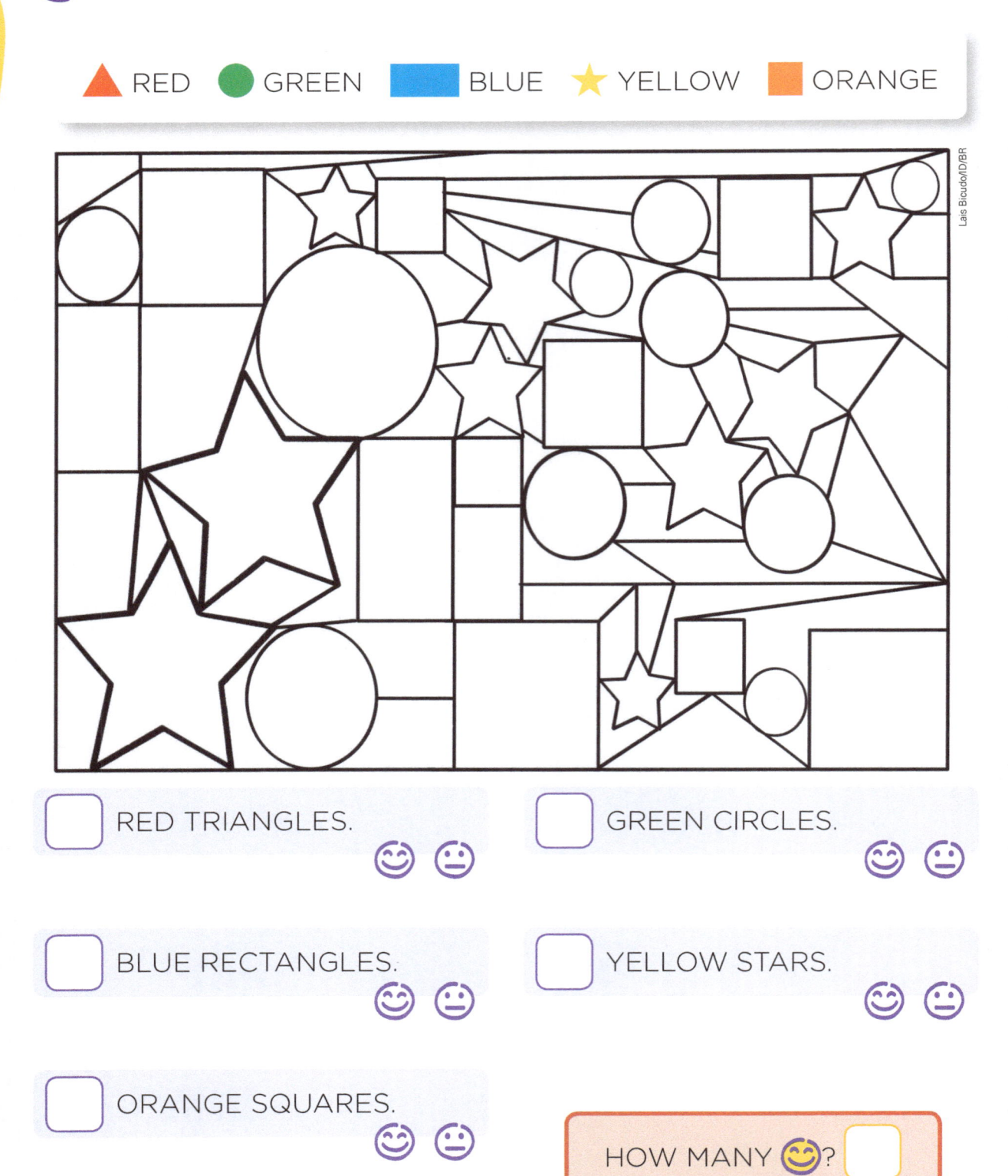

▲ RED ● GREEN ▬ BLUE ★ YELLOW ▬ ORANGE

☐ RED TRIANGLES.

☐ GREEN CIRCLES.

☐ BLUE RECTANGLES.

☐ YELLOW STARS.

☐ ORANGE SQUARES.

HOW MANY 😊 ? ☐

92 NINETY-TWO

2. LOOK AND CHECK.

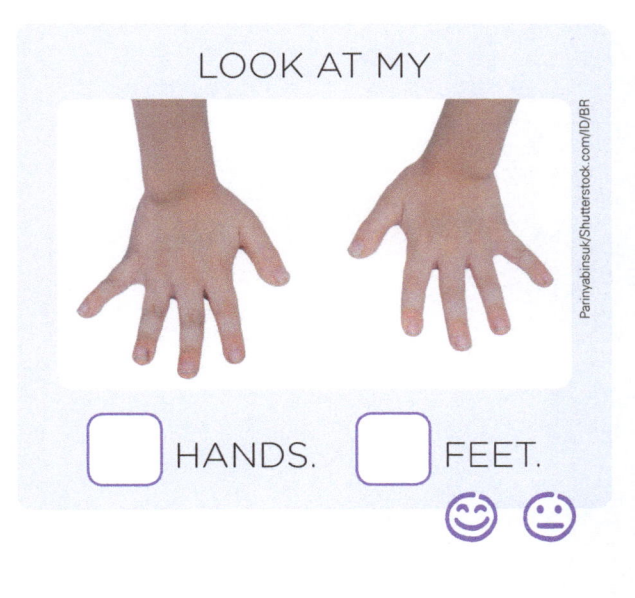

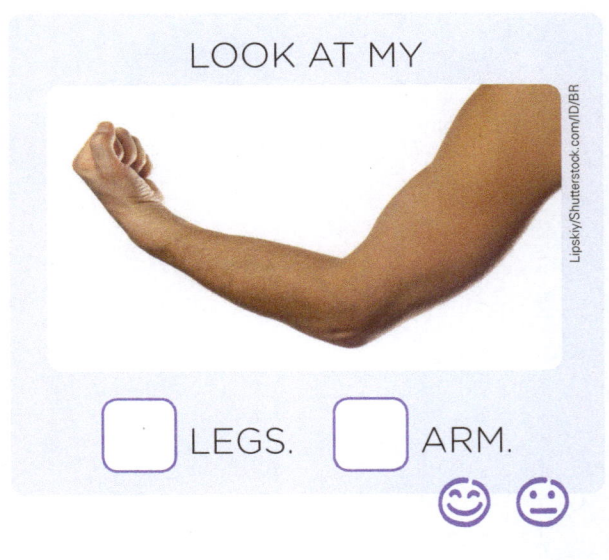

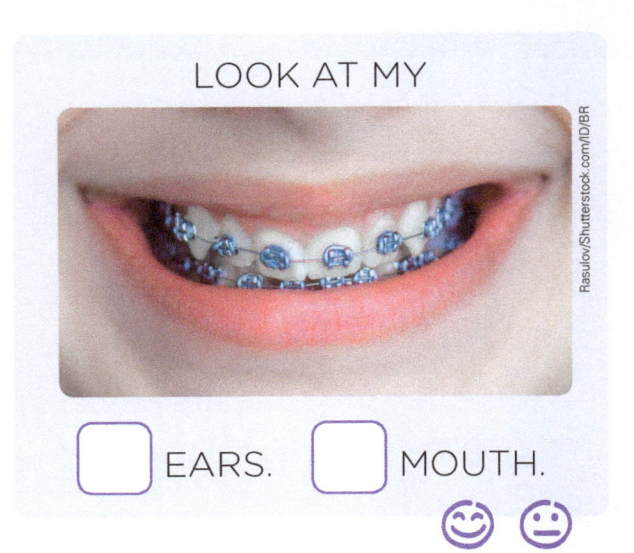

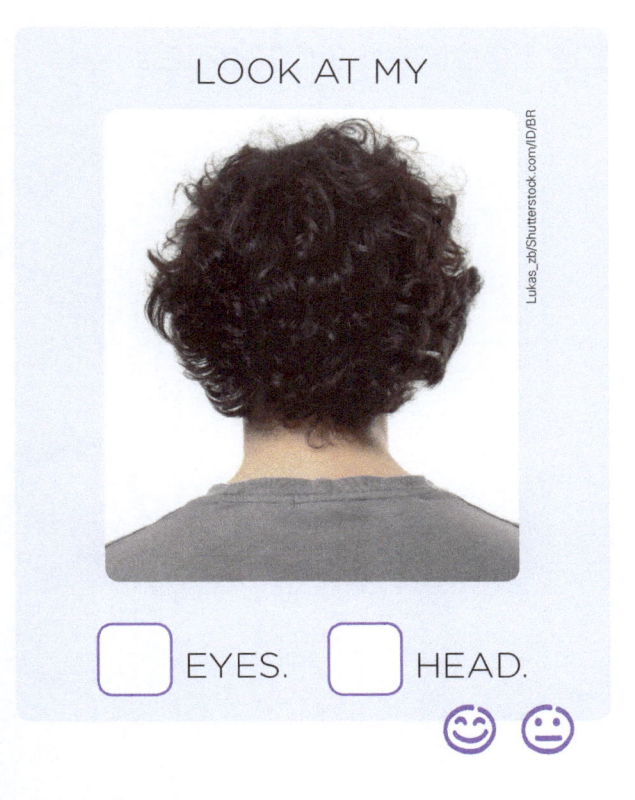

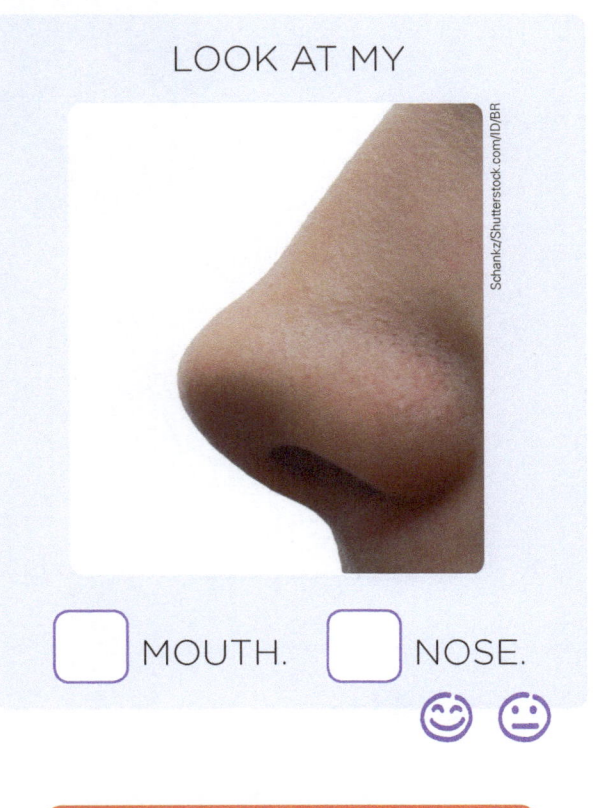

LOOK AT MY

☐ HANDS. ☐ FEET.

LOOK AT MY

☐ EYES. ☐ HEAD.

LOOK AT MY

☐ LEGS. ☐ ARM.

LOOK AT MY

☐ MOUTH. ☐ NOSE.

LOOK AT MY

☐ EARS. ☐ MOUTH.

HOW MANY 😊? ☐

NINETY-THREE 93

ANA'S FAMILY

3 LOOK AND COMPLETE.

THIS IS MY D☐D.

THIS IS MY M☐M.

THIS IS MY BR☐THER.

THIS IS ME.

THIS IS MY BABY S☐STER.

THIS IS MY GRANDP☐.

THIS IS MY GRANDM☐.

HOW MANY 😊? ☐

4 🎧 49 LISTEN AND NUMBER.

HOW MANY 😊?

GENERAL SELF-ASSESSMENT - UNITS 5-8

I CAN IMPROVE. ☐   GOOD! ☐   GREAT! ☐

NINETY-FIVE 95

WORKBOOK

UNIT 1 - AT SCHOOL

1 FIND THE PATH.

CLASSROOM

CAFETERIA

LIBRARY

96 NINETY-SIX

2 LOOK AND READ. CIRCLE **LEFT** OR **RIGHT**.

THE TOY LIBRARY IS ON THE **LEFT** / **RIGHT**.
THE GYM IS ON THE **LEFT** / **RIGHT**.
THE RESTROOM IS ON THE **LEFT** / **RIGHT**.
THE PLAYGROUND IS ON THE **LEFT** / **RIGHT**.

NINETY-SEVEN 97

UNIT 2 - SCHOOL STUFF

1 FIND AND COLOR.

ONE SCHOOL BAG   TWO BOOKS   THREE RULERS
FOUR CRAYONS   FIVE PENCILS

2 READ, COUNT AND COLOR.

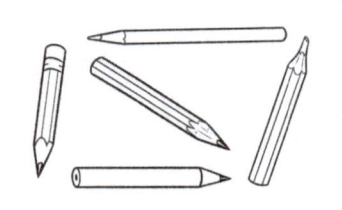

FOUR PENCILS

TWO SHARPENERS

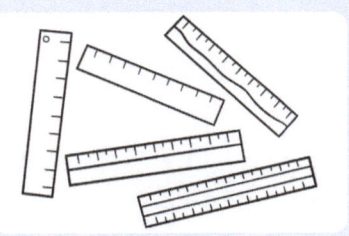

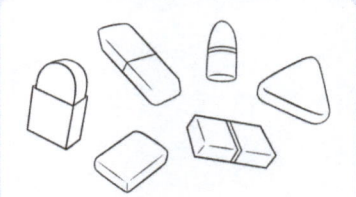

FIVE NOTEBOOKS

ONE RULER

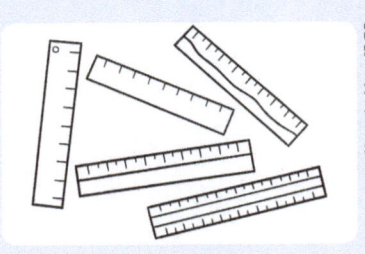

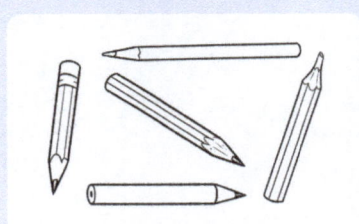

THREE PENS

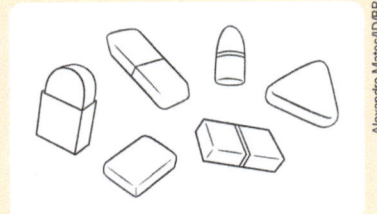

NINETY-NINE 99

UNIT 3 - COLORS ALL AROUND

1 TRACE AND COLOR.

YELLOW

BLUE

GREEN

RED

BLACK

ORANGE

PURPLE

2 LOOK AND COLOR.

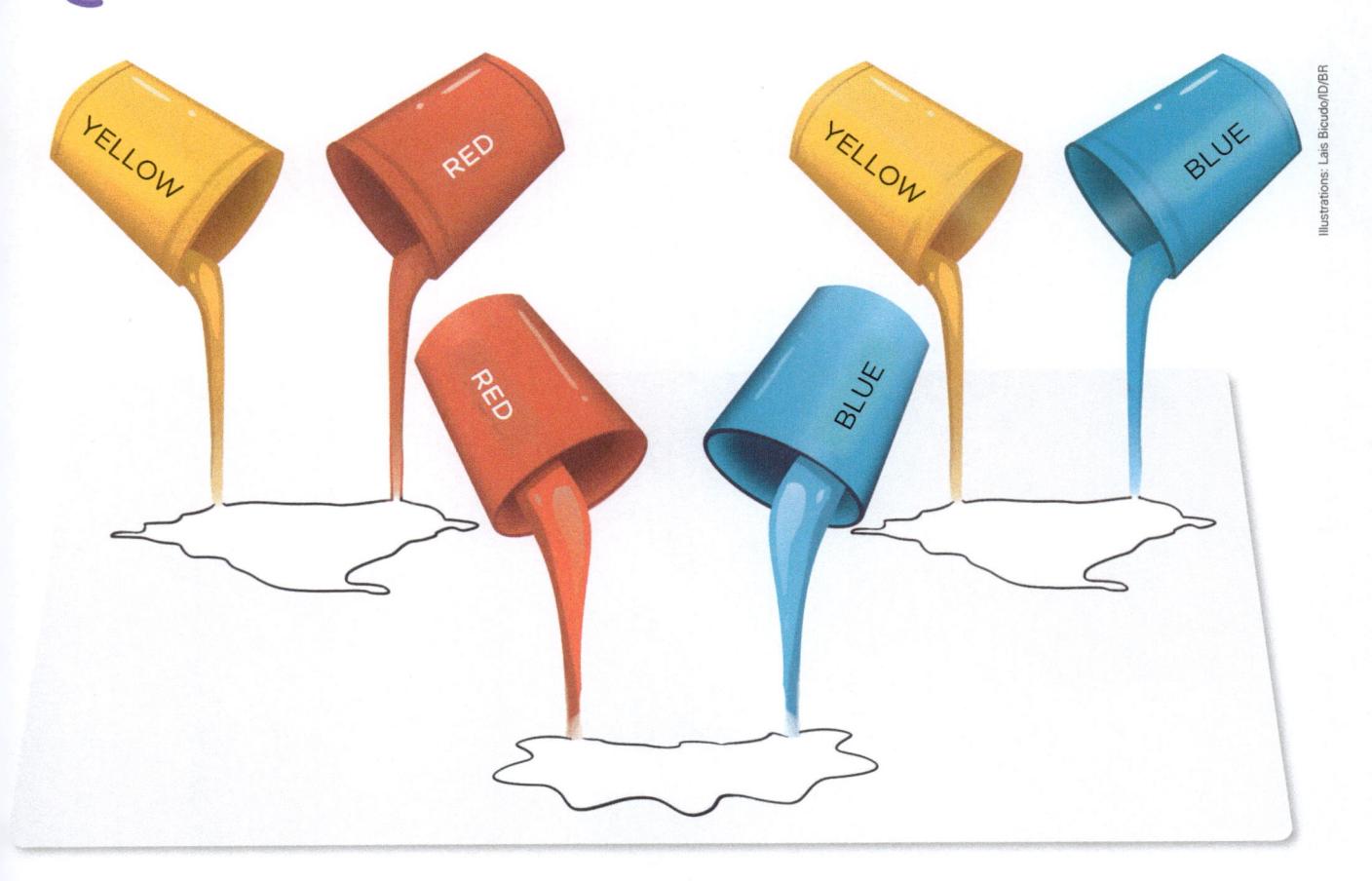

3 READ AND CIRCLE.

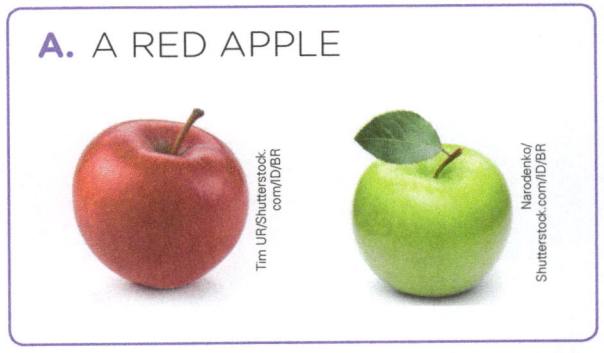

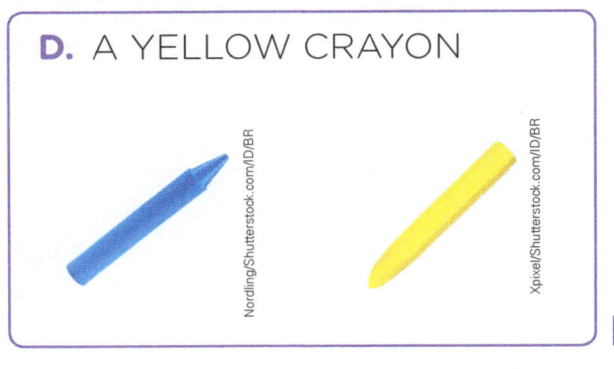

A. A RED APPLE

B. A GREEN NOTEBOOK

C. AN ORANGE BOOK

D. A YELLOW CRAYON

ONE HUNDRED AND ONE 101

UNIT 4 - THE PLAYGROUND

1 DRAW AND MATCH.

MONKEY BARS ARE FUN!

A SEESAW. LET'S PLAY!

I LOVE THE SLIDE!

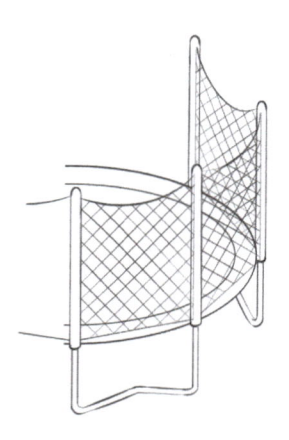

IT'S A TRAMPOLINE.

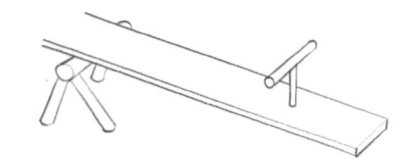

2 COLOR, FIND AND CIRCLE.

THE SWING IS **RED** / **BLUE** / **ORANGE**.
THE SEESAW IS **RED** / **BLUE** / **ORANGE**.
THE BALL IS **RED** / **BLUE** / **ORANGE**.

3 LOOK AND WRITE.

UP   DOWN

ONE HUNDRED AND THREE

UNIT 5 - SHAPES AND FUN

1 COMPLETE, COUNT AND ANSWER.

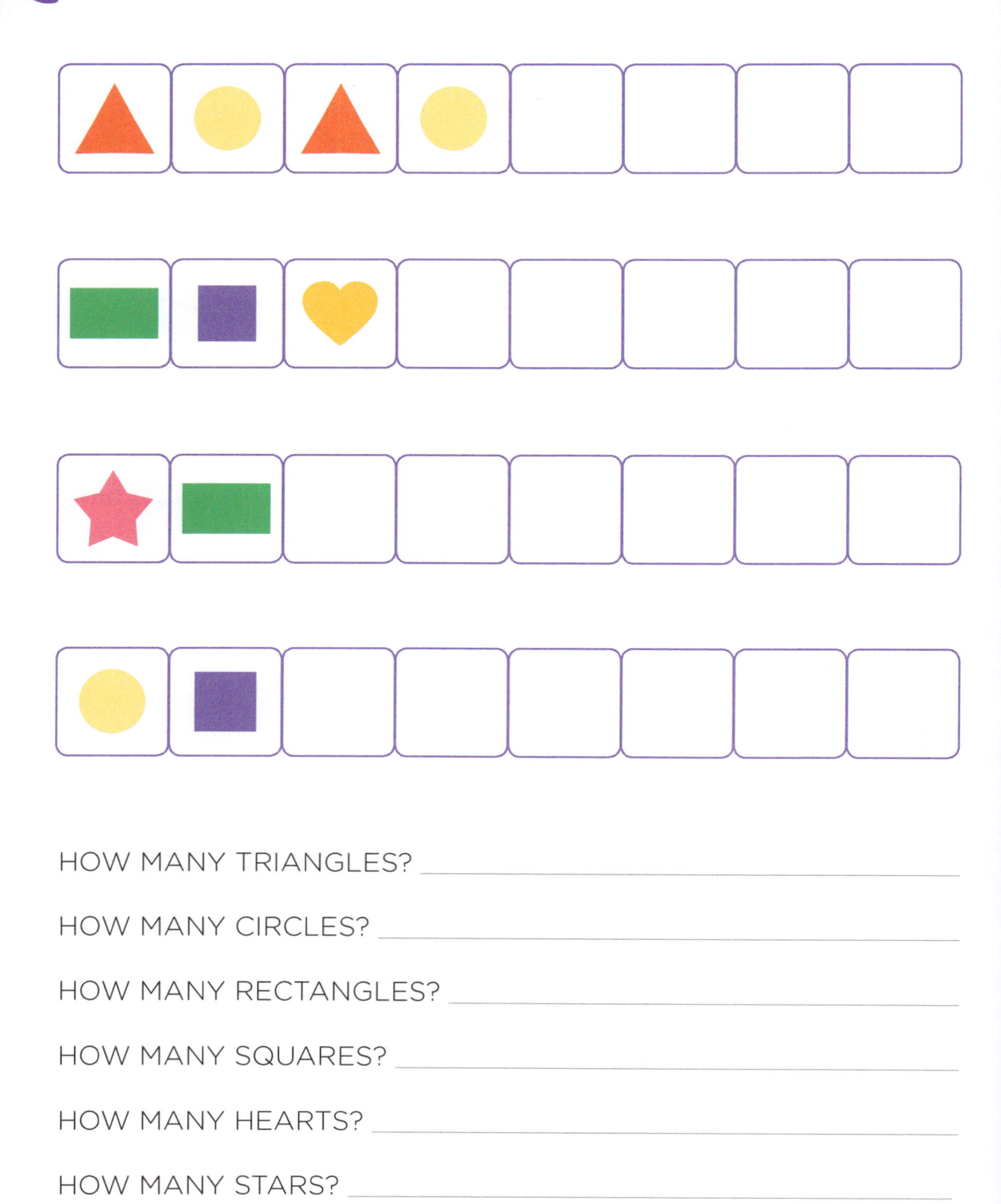

HOW MANY TRIANGLES? _____

HOW MANY CIRCLES? _____

HOW MANY RECTANGLES? _____

HOW MANY SQUARES? _____

HOW MANY HEARTS? _____

HOW MANY STARS? _____

2 READ AND CIRCLE.

A: WHAT'S THIS?
B: IT'S A RED CIRCLE.

A: WHAT'S THIS?
B: IT'S A BLUE SQUARE.

A: WHAT'S THIS?
B: IT'S A PURPLE STAR.

3 DRAW AND COLOR.

THREE BLUE RECTANGLES

SIX ORANGE HEARTS

EIGHT BLACK TRIANGLES

ONE HUNDRED AND FIVE 105

UNIT 6 - MY BODY

1 MATCH AND COLOR.

HEAD

FEET

MOUTH

HANDS

EARS

ARMS

EYES

NOSE

LEGS

2 READ AND DRAW.

LOOK AT MY HANDS!

LOOK AT MY FEET!

LOOK AT MY EYES!

LOOK AT MY MOUTH!

LOOK AT MY ARMS!

LOOK AT MY LEGS!

UNIT 7 - MY FAMILY

1 LOOK AND COMPLETE.

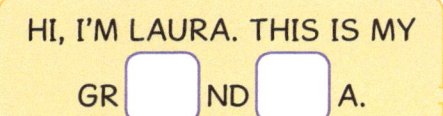

HI, I'M LAURA. THIS IS MY GR[A]ND[P]A.

THIS IS MY D[A]D.

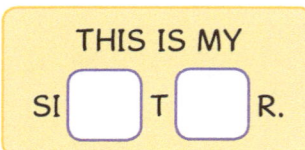

THIS IS MY SI[S]T[E]R.

THIS IS MY BA[B]Y BR[O]THE[R].

2 FIND.

MOM, WHERE ARE YOU?

HERE I AM.

GRANDMA, WHERE ARE YOU?

HERE I AM.

BROTHER, WHERE ARE YOU?

HERE I AM.

ONE HUNDRED AND NINE 109

UNIT 8 - BREAK TIME

1 READ AND CHECK.

LET'S PLAY HOPSCOTCH.

LET'S PLAY MARBLES.

LET'S PLAY TIC-TAC-TOE.

LET'S PLAY HIDE AND SEEK.

2 CONNECT THE DOTS AND COMPLETE.

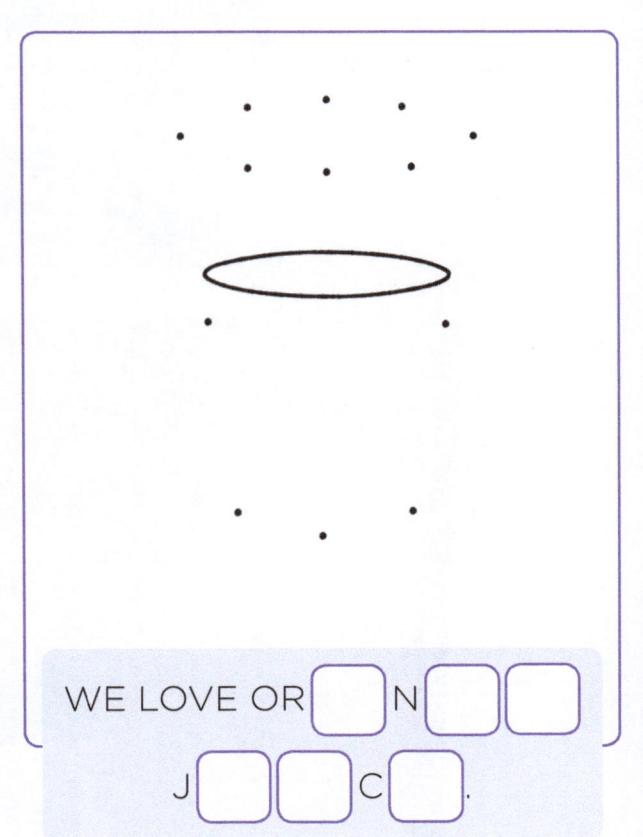

I LOVE

B [ ] N [ ] N [ ] S.

WE LOVE

[ ] PP [ ] [ ] S.

I LOVE

C [ ] [ ] K [ ] [ ] [ ] .

WE LOVE OR [ ] N [ ] [ ]

J [ ] [ ] C [ ] .

ONE HUNDRED AND ELEVEN 111

PROJECTS

UNIT 1 - AT SCHOOL

PLACES AT MY SCHOOL

MATERIALS

PAPER OR POSTER BOARD

ART SUPPLIES

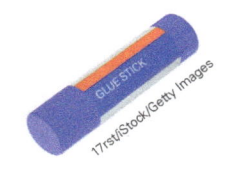

GLUE

SCISSORS

UNIT 2 - SCHOOL STUFF
LABELING STUFF

MATERIALS

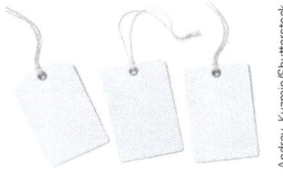

STRIPS OF PAPER

MARKERS

COLORED PENCILS

MASKING TAPE

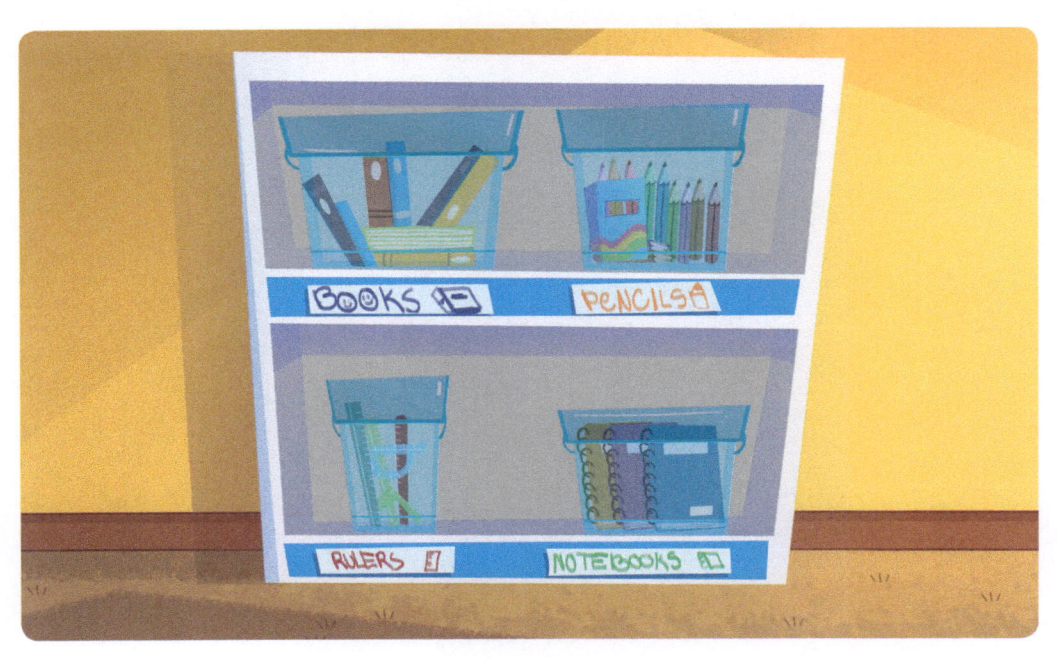

UNIT 3 - COLORS ALL AROUND

THE COLOR BOOK

MATERIALS

PAPER

CRAYONS

COLORED PENCILS

YARN

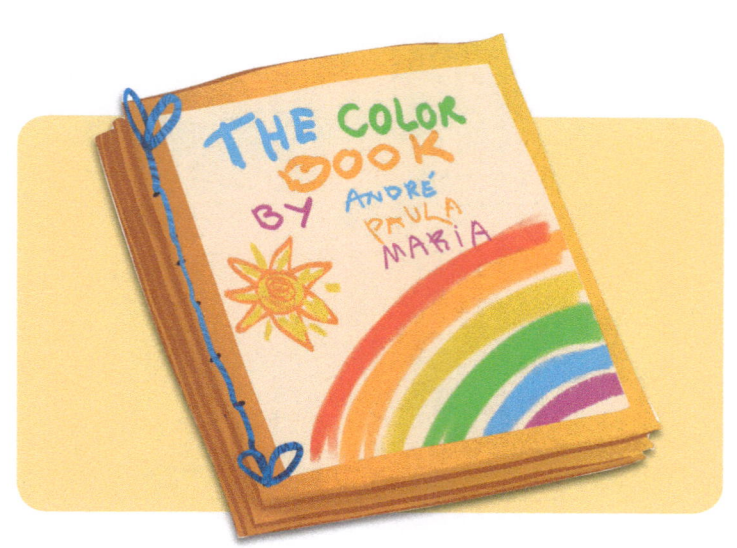

114 ONE HUNDRED AND FOURTEEN

UNIT 4 - THE PLAYGROUND

PLAYING IN THE PLAYGROUND

MATERIALS

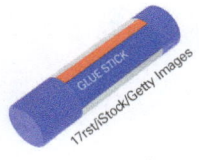

COLORED PAPER

ART SUPPLIES

GLUE

MASKING TAPE

MONKEY BARS

SLIDE

SWING

ONE HUNDRED AND FIFTEEN 115

UNIT 5 - SHAPES AND FUN
SHAPE COLLAGE

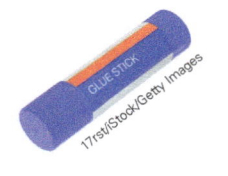

MATERIALS

POSTER BOARD COLORED PAPER GLUE SCISSORS

116 ONE HUNDRED AND SIXTEEN

UNIT 6 - MY BODY
MODELING A CLAY PERSON

MATERIALS

PAPER

MODELING CLAY

STICKS

ONE HUNDRED AND SEVENTEEN 117

UNIT 7 - MY FAMILY
FAMILY PORTRAIT
MATERIALS

PAPER   ART SUPPLIES   GLUE   SCISSORS   MAGAZINES

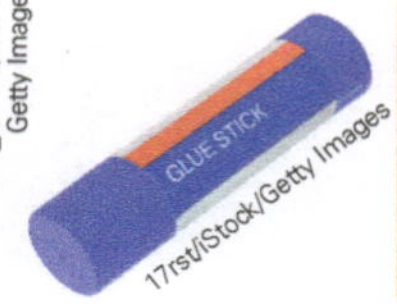

118 ONE HUNDRED AND EIGHTEEN

UNIT 8 - BREAK TIME
GAME DAY

MATERIALS

PAPER OR POSTER BOARD

MARKERS

COLORED PENCILS

ONE HUNDRED AND NINETEEN 119

CLASSROOM LANGUAGE

ACT OUT

CHECK

CIRCLE

CLOSE YOUR BOOKS

COLOR

COMPLETE

CROSS OUT

DANCE

DRAW

FIND

120 ONE HUNDRED AND TWENTY

GLUE

CONNECT THE DOTS

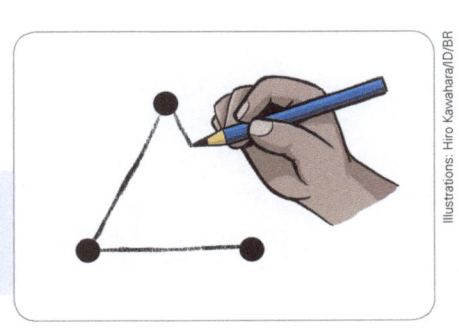

LISTEN

LOOK

MATCH

NUMBER

OPEN YOUR BOOKS

PLAY

POINT

RAISE YOUR HAND

READ

SAY

SHOW

SING

SIT DOWN

STAND UP

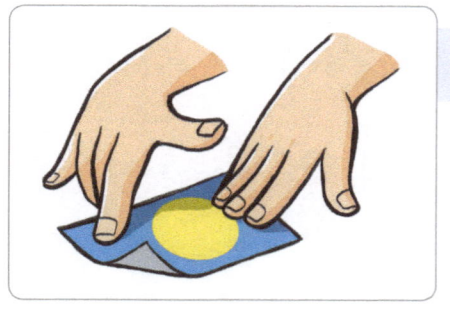

STICK

TOUCH

TRACE

WRITE

GLOSSARY

WELCOME - HELLO, COME IN!

BOY — GIRL — SCHOOL — STUDENT — TEACHER

UNIT 1 - AT SCHOOL

CAFETERIA — CLASSROOM — GYM

LIBRARY — PLAYGROUND — RESTROOM

TOY LIBRARY — LEFT/RIGHT

CONTEÚDO NA VERSÃO DIGITAL

ONE HUNDRED AND TWENTY-THREE 123

GLOSSARY

UNIT 2 - SCHOOL STUFF

SHARPENER
RULER
SCHOOL BAG
ERASER
PEN
PENCIL
BOOK
CRAYON
NOTEBOOK

ONE TWO THREE FOUR FIVE

UNIT 3 - COLORS ALL AROUND

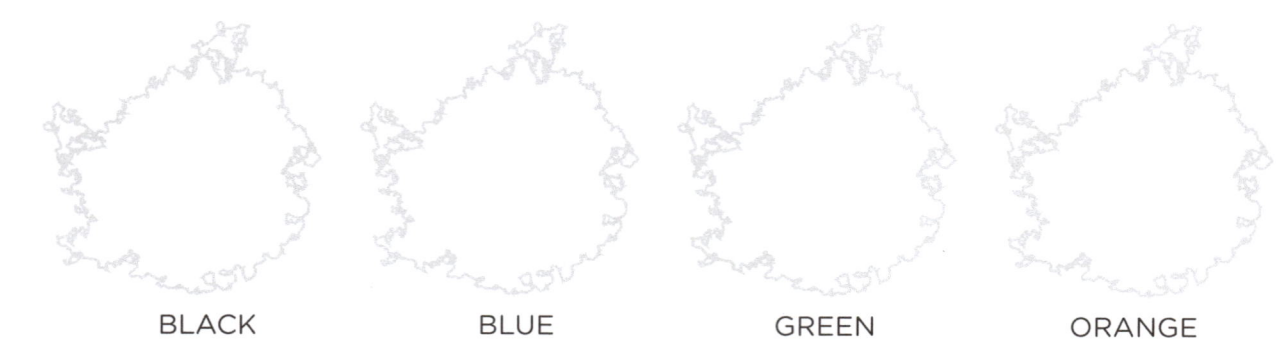

BLACK BLUE GREEN ORANGE

PURPLE RED WHITE YELLOW

UNIT 3 - COLORS ALL AROUND

SKY
SUN
APPLE
GRASS

UNIT 4 - THE PLAYGROUND

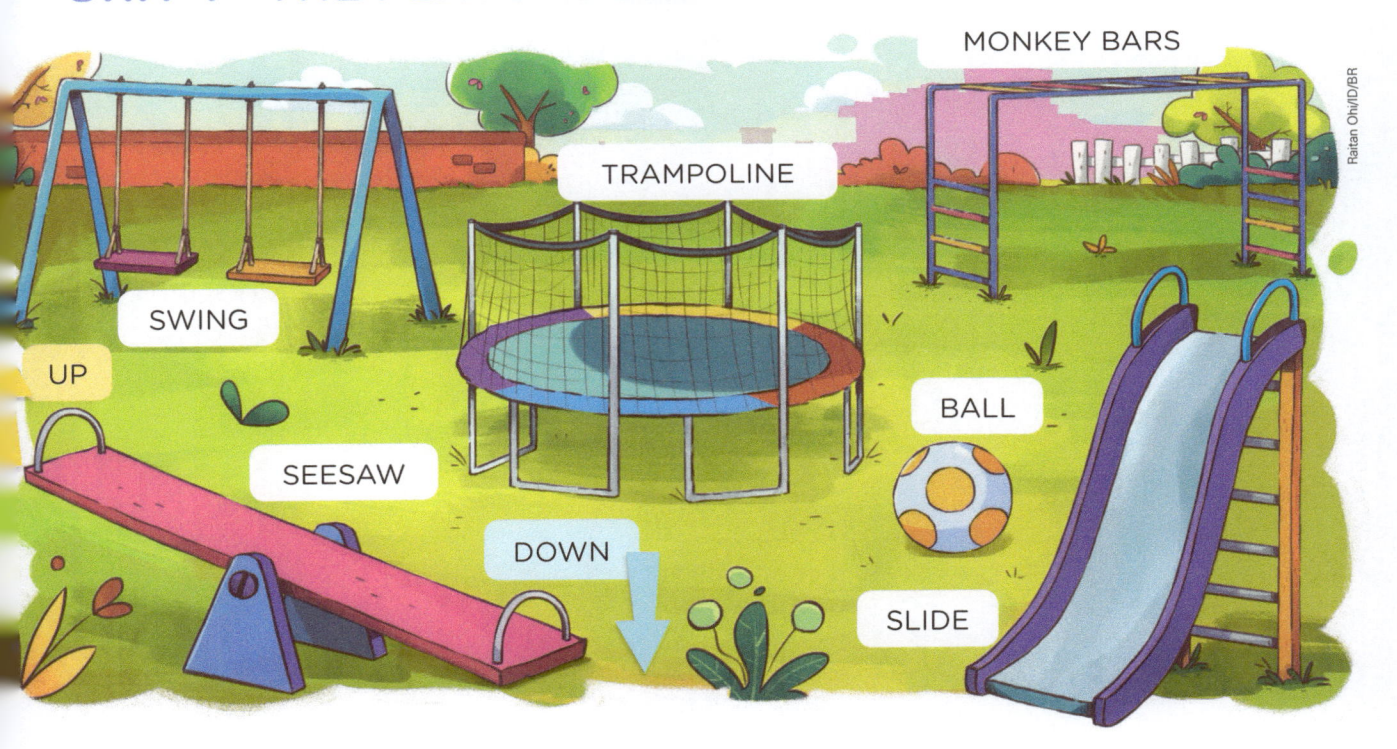

MONKEY BARS
TRAMPOLINE
SWING
UP
SEESAW
DOWN
BALL
SLIDE

ONE HUNDRED AND TWENTY-FIVE 125

GLOSSARY

UNIT 5 - SHAPES AND FUN

CIRCLE   HEART   RECTANGLE   SQUARE

STAR   TRIANGLE   HULA HOOP

SIX   SEVEN   EIGHT   NINE   TEN

UNIT 6 - MY BODY

HEAD
EYES
NOSE
MOUTH
EARS
ARMS
HANDS
LEGS
FEET

ARM
EAR
EYE
FOOT
HAND
LEG

HEARING
SIGHT
SMELL
TASTE
TOUCH

GLOSSARY

UNIT 7 - MY FAMILY

JOANA'S FAMILY

JOANA

- GRANDPA
- DAD
- MOM
- BABY
- GRANDMA
- BROTHER
- SISTER

UNIT 8 - BREAK TIME

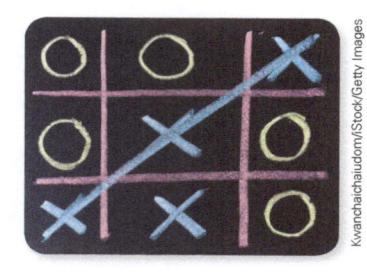

- COOKIE
- HIDE AND SEEK
- HOPSCOTCH
- MARBLES
- ORANGE JUICE
- TIC-TAC-TOE
- WATER

PRESS OUTS

PAGES 41, 60, 71, 81 • DICE, PAWNS AND CARDS

INSTRUCTION

GLUE HERE

ONE HUNDRED AND TWENTY-NINE 129

PRESS OUTS

PAGES 20, 26 • **PUZZLE AND CARDS**

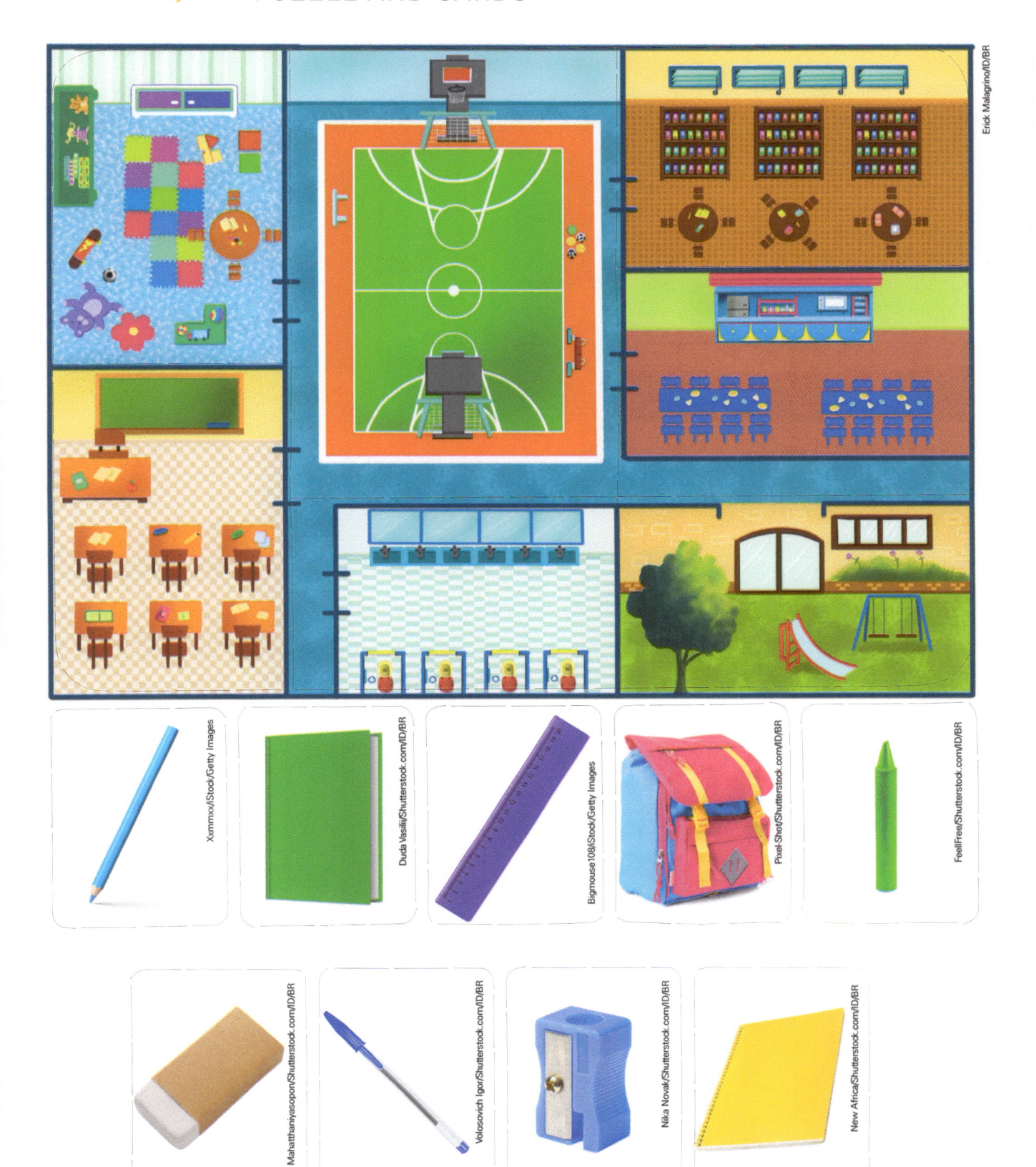

ONE HUNDRED AND THIRTY-ONE 131

PRESS OUTS

PAGES 44, 66 • **PUZZLE AND CARDS**

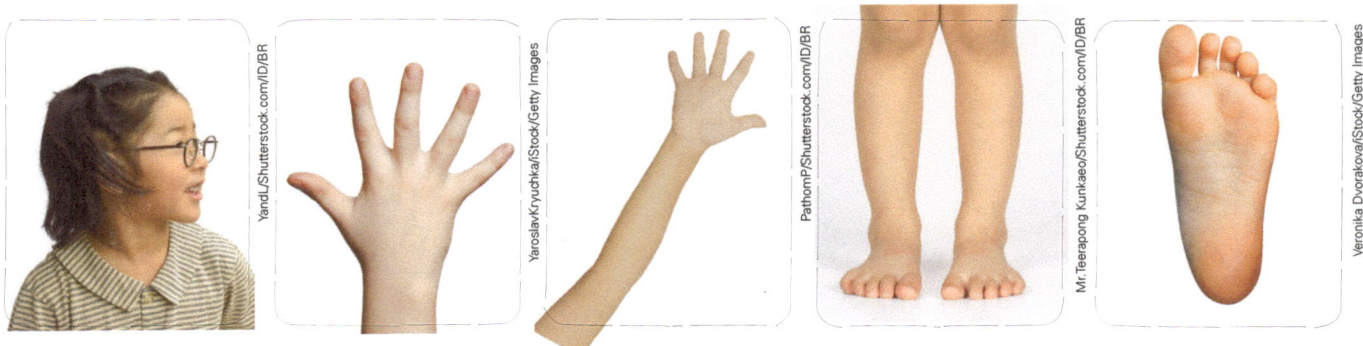

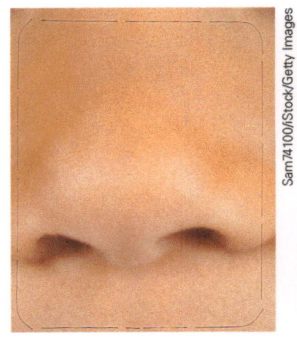

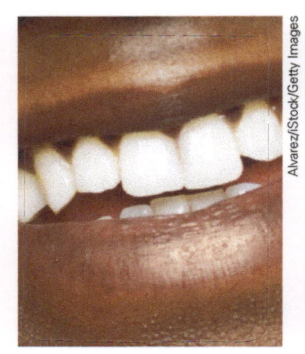

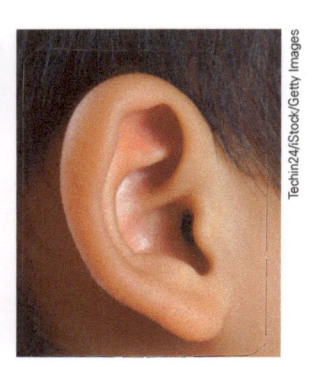

ONE HUNDRED AND THIRTY-THREE 133

PRESS OUTS

PAGES 78, 82 • **FINGER PUPPETS AND CARDS**

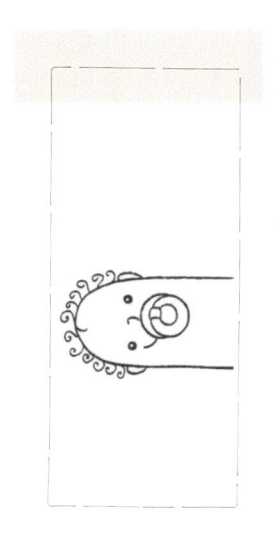

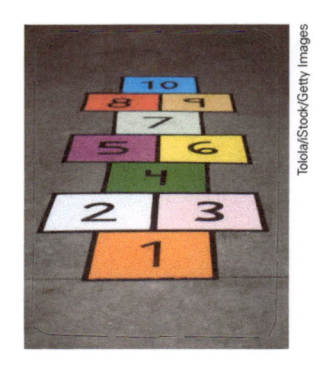

ONE HUNDRED AND THIRTY-FIVE 135

STICKERS

PAGE 15 • LISTEN, STICK AND SAY.
WELCOME

PAGE 18 • LISTEN AND STICK.
UNIT 1

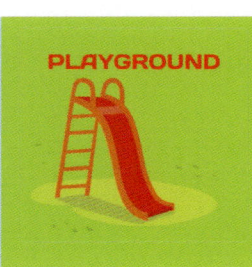

PAGE 27 • LISTEN, STICK AND SAY.
UNIT 2

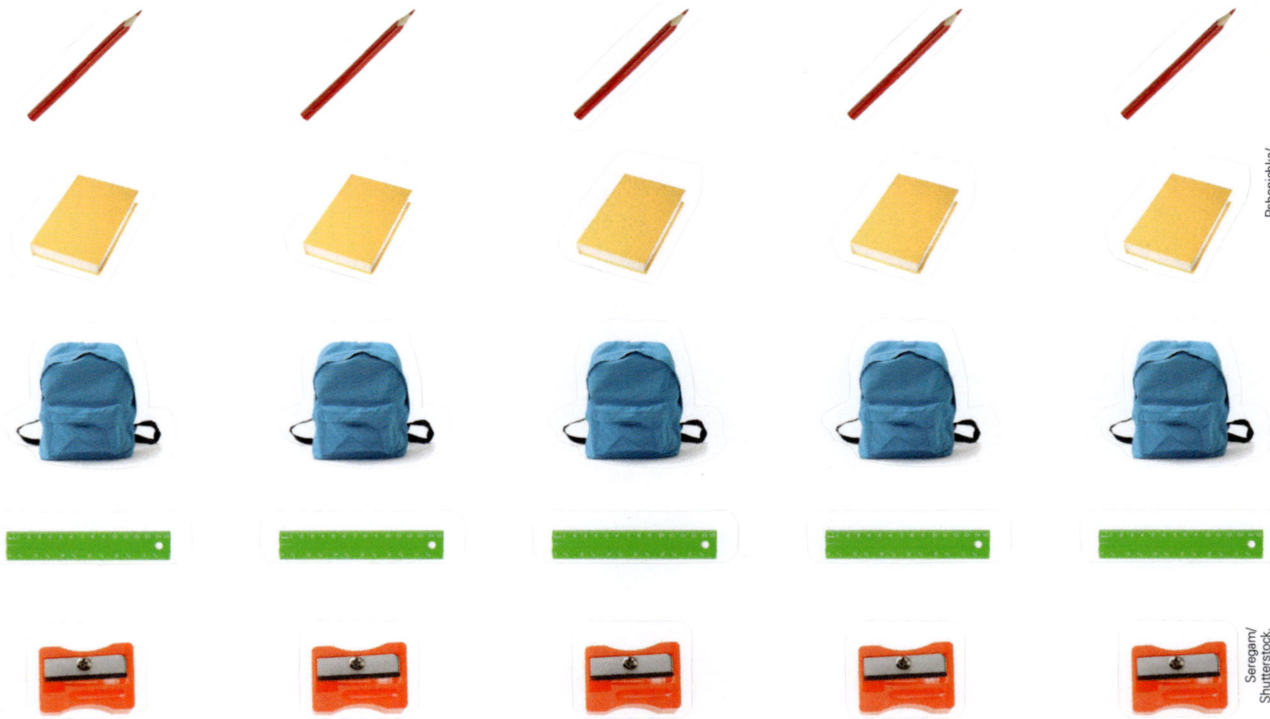

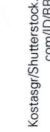

ONE HUNDRED AND THIRTY-SEVEN **137**

STICKERS

PAGE 37 • STICK AND ACT OUT.

UNIT 3

PAGE 47 • LISTEN, CIRCLE AND STICK.

UNIT 4

SLIDE

SEESAW

SWING

STUDENT

PAGE 48 • LOOK AND STICK.

UNIT 4

ONE HUNDRED AND THIRTY-NINE 139

STICKERS

PAGE 59 • LISTEN, STICK AND SAY.

UNIT 5

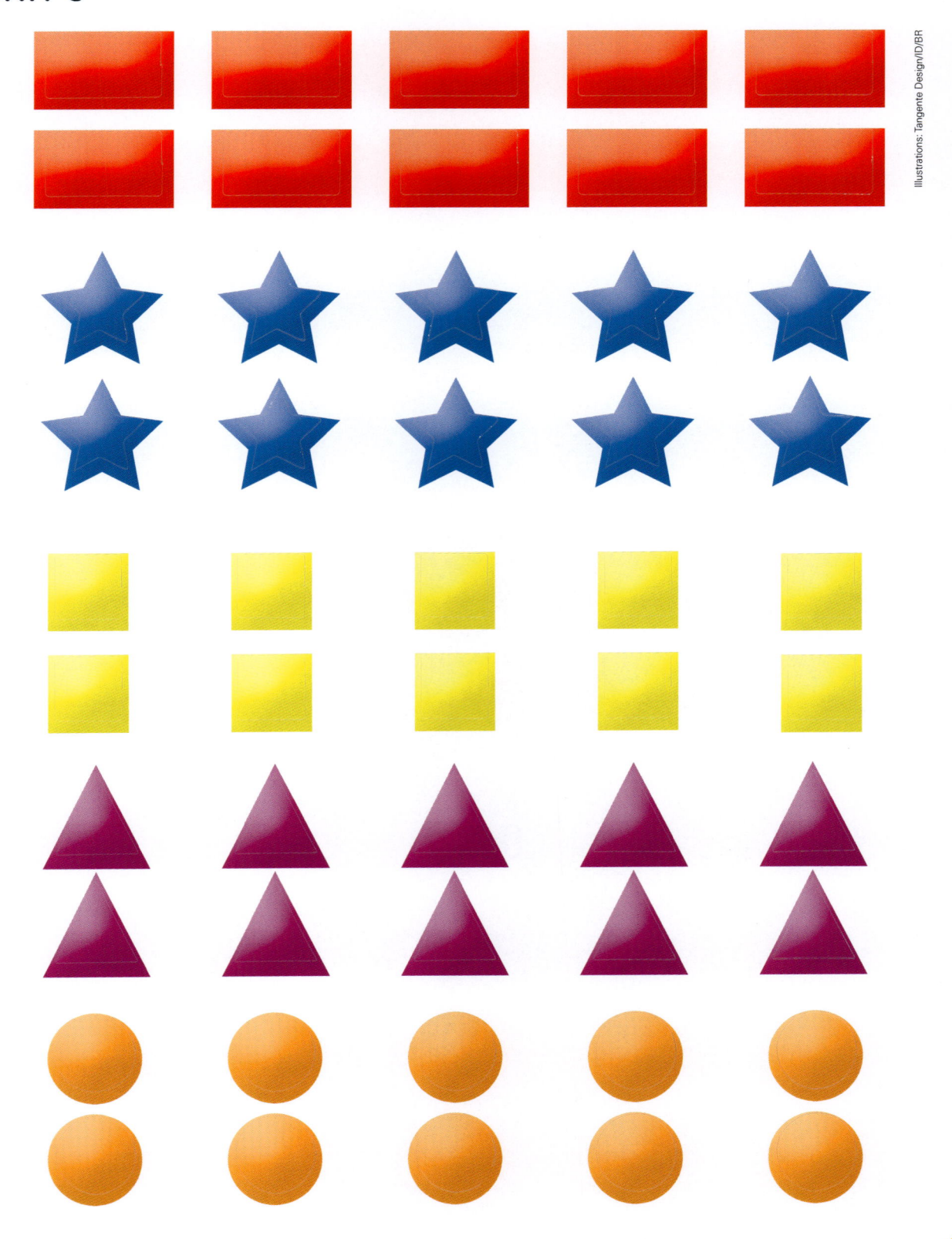

ONE HUNDRED AND FORTY-ONE 141

STICKERS

PAGE 66 • LOOK, STICK AND SAY.

UNIT 6

ARMS   LEGS

HANDS   FEET   HEAD

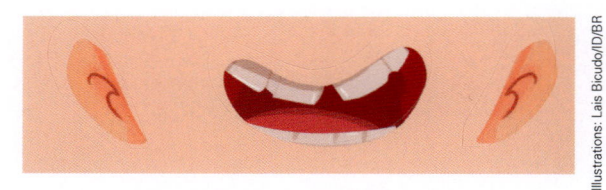

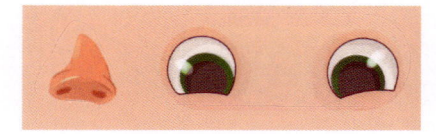

PAGE 76 • LISTEN AND STICK.

UNIT 7

GRANDMA   DAD   BABY SISTER   BROTHER

PAGE 88 • LOOK AND STICK.

UNIT 8

ONE HUNDRED AND FORTY-THREE   143